‖ Mahabharat ‖

Retold by
Raja Mangalvedhekar

JYOTSNA PRAKASHAN

Published in Marathi as
Sulabh Mahabharat
English rendering by
Sharad Mahabal

Published by:
Milind L. Paranjape
Jyotsna Prakashan
'Dhavalgiri'
430/31 Shaniwar Peth
Pune 411 030

Cover & Illustrations
Gopal Nandurkar

© Jyotsna Prakashan, 2002

First Published: August 2002
Second Edition: June 2005
Reprint : 2008

Printed by:
S.K. Printers
205 Shaniwar Peth
Pune 411 030

Price Rs. 75/-

ISBN 81-7925-052-0

JYOTSNA PRAKASAHN
Mumbai office:
Mohan Building
162 J.Shankarsheth Marg
Girgaum, Mumbai 400 004

‖ Saga of the Kuru Dynasty ‖

Shounak's ashram was in the midst of Naimisharanya, a dense jungle.

Shounak was a renowned sage. Imparting knowledge, learning new things and performing yagnas formed important part of his daily tasks.

Once Shounak began at his ashram, a yagna that was to go on for over a decade – twelve years, to be precise. Sages from various places gathered at his ashram to perform the yagna.

One day as the sages were relaxing after work, a person named Sootaputra Souti arrived. His visit was unexpected. Souti was well-known for giving discourses. It was a sheer pleasure to hear him narrate tales from mythology or detailed accounts of events of past. The sages were glad to receive Souti. Shounak offered him a seat, and was also served milk.

Souti greeted the sages and said," I hope your yagnas are going well."

"Yes, of course and our yagnas too are taking place without any hindrance. But tell us first, Souti, from where have you come from now? Where were you all these days?" asked a veteran sage.

Souti replied humbly,

"I have come from King Janameyjaya, the son of King Parikshita, O wise ones! I was with him all these days. During the *Sarp-satra** he had organized an excellent programme each evening. You may have heard of it."

"And what was the programme?"

"Vaishampayan, the disciple of Lord Vyas, used to narrate the saga of King Janameyjaya's forefathers for the benefit of the king. I too heard the grand tale."

"I see! Souti, then tell us all the story that you found so interesting."

All those assembled supported this idea and they requested Souti to narrate the story.

Souti honoured their wish and explained,

"O Sages! This story is a narration by Vyas of the glorious history, right from the days of Daksh Prajapati. That is why it is known as 'Mahabharat'. Some also call it 'Jaya'. "

Introducing thus, Souti narrated the history of the dynasty of Kurus of Hastinapur.

|| King Shantanu ||

It happened more than a thousand years ago, in the city of Hastinapur. Hastinapur was the capital of the Kuru dynasty. Bharat*, the brave son of King Dushyant, ruled from here. Those days, the city was called Asandivrat or Brahmagiri. The last of the six kings who ruled after Bharat was called Hastin. It was after him that the city came to be known as Hastinapur.

Hastin was brave and was related from his mother's side to the Ikshvaku dynasty of Ayodhya. Thus, he inherited the rich legacy of two great dynasties.

Hastin was succeeded by Prateep who had three sons – Devapi, Balhik and Shantanu.

As Prateep became old, in the court he expressed his wish to hand over the throne to his son. The eldest son, Devapi, would be the crown prince, as per custom. But a veteran courtier rose to object to his coronation stating Devapi has leprosy and should not be crowned as the subjects would not approve of a leper king.

Devapi also expressed, "I do not wish to rule."

Immediately afterwards, the second son Balhik also rose and declared his reluctance to carry on thus:

"I have heard that the revered land of our forefathers was across the river Sindhu (Indus) long ago. I wish to conquer that land and seek your permission, my Lord."

Thus the remaining son, Shantanu, was eventually made the King of Hastinapur.

Shantanu was a brave king and good administrator. Those days, the kings used to be Kshatriyas and thus Shantanu was fond of hunting. For hunting helped the skills in archery and also developed courage.

Once as Shantanu was on the banks of the Ganga, visiting shrines and ashrams of sages, he spotted a beautiful woman. She was as pretty as a picture. Her extraordinary beauty enchanted the king who asked,

"Who are you, O fair one?"

"I am called Ganga," she said.

"Well! I am Shantanu, King of Hastinapur," he introduced himself. "I am so totally enchanted by your beauty that I cannot bear any more to live without you! Will you marry me, O the doe-eyed one?"

Upon this question of the king , Ganga said,

"I shall fulfill your wish and marry you, only on one condition."

"Of course! What is the condition?"

"Though I become your wife, you cannot keep me in any bondage. I shall be free to behave just as I please – you shall not hinder me. The moment you break this rule, I shall be free to leave you."

"I agree to abide by your condition," the king assured.

Ganga and Shantanu became a happy man-and-wife. In that bliss days flew, months and months and years passed.

During this period, Ganga had seven children. But she would drown each infant in the river Ganga as soon as it was born. Seeing every baby perish at its birth in such a cruel manner, Shantanu was deeply grieved. But he kept mum as agreed. When the eighth child was born, and Ganga set out to drown him too, Shantanu could not keep quiet any longer. He said, "Stop killing one's own babies like this! You must be having a rock for your heart! What do you gain this way? Who are you, after all, you devil?"

Ganga stopped and said, "I understand your heart agonizes by the loss of the sons. I shall keep your wish and let this son live. But this is the end of our life together. Let me tell you about myself. I am Ganga, the river of heavens. Due to a curse by Vashishth, the Ashta-Vasus* were doomed to take birth on the earth from my womb; they

were born as our sons. Now I'll look after the last one while he is young. He shall add to your renown, when he grows up."

Saying so, Ganga vanished.

Stuck by grief at this turn of events, Shantanu returned home. He somehow engaged himself in looking after his people as a duty.

Days passed, and when Shantanu went to the riverside for hunting, he found the water-level too low. He was surprised. He then noticed that upstream a bonny boy held up the flow of the river with his arrows!

Quite surprised, Shantanu set out to ask the boy about it. But the boy simply laughed and disappeared in the vast expanse of the Ganga.

The king was all the more surprised. But then remembering the history, he exclaimed in confusion,

"O Ganga! Tell me what this is all about!"

Reading the vibrations of the king's mind, Ganga manifested herself and said, "This is Gangadutt, your eighth son to whom I gave birth. I have looked after him. Parashuram has taught him martial knowledge; and he has studied the *Vedas* from Sage Vashishth. I now hand over this great warrior to you."

The king was overjoyed. He returned to Hastinapur with his son, and made him the crown prince, after naming him Deovrat.

With his virtues and valour, Deovrat won the approbation and admiration of the old and young.

‖ *Satyavati* ‖

Days went on and about four years passed. Once, while wandering along the riverside, Shantanu smelt an extraordinary fragrance. Oh! It was quite pleasing and winning over all mental faculties, and yet unnamed. It was never felt before. Tracing the origin of the scent, the king reached the riverside. There he found a young fisherwoman of exceptional beauty playing with the waters.

Approaching her, the king asked,

"What is your name, O beauty?"

"Satyavati."

"Which family do you come from?"

"I am fisherman Daash's daughter."

As Satyavati spoke, waves of that fragrance danced around her. Like a flower, Satyavati had the special blessing of the fragrance. Earlier too, Satyavati was as pretty as now but her body smelled of fish. People called her Matsyagandha.

Nobody dared to go near her fearing the stink.

But this changed when Sage Paraashar crossed the river Ganga in her boat. Paraashar was quite pleased with Satyavati. By the virtue of the power of his penance, he eliminated the evil smell from Satyavati's body and made her fragrant instead. As this sweet smell began to reach far and wide, she came to be known as Yojangandha*.

Around this time, Satyavati gave birth to a son by Paraashar. The dark complexioned boy was born on an island in the river, and thus came to be known as Krishnadvaipaayan*. The boy was later renowned as Vedvyas, the Maharshi.

But all this became a part of history when King Shantanu met Satyavati. He asked, "Will you marry me, O Scented One?"

Satyavati was quite abashed at this. She said, "Please seek the permission of my father for any such proposal."

The king called on the fisherman Daash to seek his daughter's hand. The fisherman was very happy but at the same time he felt hesitant and shy. He remarked, "While we are simple fishermen, you are kings. You may forget my daughter in a matter of days."

"I promise you Daash that your daughter shall always be my favourite queen," the king answered.

"You may well keep your word and see that Satyavati is contented and happy. But the child that she'll bear will certainly suffer because your son Deovrat shall succeed you on the throne as king. Satyavati's children, due to being younger, shall have to remain under his thumb. Instead, if you promise that Satyavati's son shall be the king after you, I shall willingly marry Satyavati to you."

Shantanu was in a fix. He was in two minds: whether to honour Deovrat's right or agree with Satyavati's father's wishes to win her?

Finally Shantanu made up his mind with a hard resolve, "No, I cannot promise it for the sake of Satyavati. That would mean trampling Deovrat's birthright. I cannot be unjust."

Shantanu returned to the palace in gloom. He had stood true to the side of justice, but had failed to get Satyavati. He remained depressed all the while. He could no longer concentrate on the state affairs. He would lie sleepless night after night; lose weight, day by day.

Deovrat came to know the cause of his father's sorrow through the Prime Minister. Hearing of it, Deovrat went to Daash and said, "For the sake of my father's happiness, I can even sacrifice my life. What of the throne and its power then?"

"You are great, Prince," said Daash.

"But this is not the end of my worry. You may keep the word. But your children will fight with my grandchildren. Who knows? Why taste the bitter pill of this relation? We will merely be causing misery to the next generations. Let us drop the idea."

Upon this, Deovrat fell silent for a while, but later solemnly replied, "I am prepared for the biggest sacrifice for my father's happiness. Gods are witnesses and I vow that I shall remain unmarried, and observe celibacy all my life. All issues born to your daughter shall be looked after by me as brothers. I shall protect these brothers and their children all my life!"

Due to this solemn and severe vow, Deovrat came to be known as Bheeshma.

‖ Growth of the Kuru family ‖

Shantanu was quite pleased with his son Deovrat; for he had made a towering sacrifice for his father's sake. He granted him a boon; he could hold back death and die only at will.

After marrying Satyavati, Shantanu spent his days happily, in great contentment.

Satyavati gave birth to two sons of the king – the elder was named Chitraangad and the younger, Vichitraveerya. Bheeshma saw to it that his brothers received proper education right since the beginning. When these brothers were still young, Shantanu breathed his last.

Bheeshma made Chitraangad the king. Chitraangad was a brave warrior as well as a skilful administrator. He expanded the Kuru empire by invading many kingdoms and conquering them. However, Chitraangad was slain in a mysterious battle with the Gandharvs.

Subsequently, Vichitraveerya became king. But not only was Vichitraveerya immature due to the young age, but he also lacked efficiency. Bheeshma thus looked after the state in the name of Vichitraveerya, with the permission of Satyavati.

After a few days, Bheeshma learnt that King Kashiraj was marrying his three daughters by the *svayamvar** tradition. Vichitraveerya was by then of marriageable age. After consulting Satyavati, Bheeshma took Vichitraveerya to the *svayamvar*.

Kashiraj's three daughters – Amba, Ambika and Ambalika – proceeded through the *svayamvar* pandal observing every prince. As they passed by Bheeshma, they commented on his old age and rejected him. The assembled kings mocked and laughed at this incident. An angry Bheeshma forcefully put the three princesses in his chariot and challenged all the kings to fight with him. A mighty battle followed. Bheeshma single-handedly defeated all the kings and returned with the three princesses to Hastinapur.

Of the three princesses, Amba urged Bheeshma, "I have chosen Shalva, the King of Soubh, as my husband. Allow me to go to him." Bheeshma consented to her request, and then the other two princesses – Ambika and Ambalika – were married to Vichitraveerya with great fanfare.

Some time thus passed happily. Satyavati was quite engrossed with the two daughters-in-law. But, suddenly, it was found that Vichitraveerya had contracted tuberculosis. Despite all treatment, he succumbed to the disease.

Satyavati was plunged into grief – she had lost her husband and both sons. Moreover since there was no son from both the daughters-in-law, the lineage was about to end. Quite grieved, Satyavati mentioned the gloomy prospect to Bheeshma as he could change it. He replied,

"Mother, any deviation from my vow is unthinkable. You may ask for anything else."

Satyavati was aware of Bheeshma's great resolve. She told him about her son born in the boat from Sage Paraashar.

Bheeshma said,

"It is heartening to know that Maharshi Vyas is a son of yours. You can very well take his help in the present crisis."

Satyavati revoked Vedvyas within her mind and soon he readily stood before her.

"What makes you command my presence?" Vyas asked.

Satyavati then narrated the situation and expressed the desire that the withering of the lineage should be stopped.

"If you wish so, I can help the Kuru line to continue by the *niyog** method of reproduction."

Consequently, Ambika and Ambalika bore Dhritarashtra and Pandu from Vyas. Since Ambika was afraid of Vyas' ferocious looks, and had closed her eyes when she met him, Dhritarashtra was born blind. And as terror had made Ambalika pale, her son Pandu too was pale as if affected by some wasting disease. A maid was also sent by Ambika to Vyas; she however gave birth to a healthy, normal, wise son named Vidur.

Bheeshma brought up Dhritarashtra and Pandu with great love and care; and educated them well. He also got them married when they were of age. Gaandhari, the princess of the Gandhar country, became Dhritarashtra's wife. When she learnt that he was born blind, she too tied her own eyes with a strip of cloth for the entire lifetime.

Pandu married Kunti, the daughter of the King Kuntibhoj. She was blessed by Sage Durvas with a boon. By chanting a particular mantra, a particular deity would appear and bless her with a son having the special characteristics of that deity; that was Durvas' promise. With natural curiosity, she had chanted the mantra before marriage and invoked the Sun-god, Surya. Though a maiden, she gave birth to a son who was brave and fiery like the Sun. To avoid stigma and censure by people, she quietly placed the infant in a wicker basket and sent the basket off down a stream. As the baby floated down the stream, Adhirath, a chariot driver by profession, saw the basket and took the child home, since he had none of his own.

The throne of Hastinapur, by rights, would have been Dhritarashtra's. But since he was blind, his younger brother Pandu was crowned as king.

Pandu had also married another princess – Madree. This princess of the Madra country was very pretty and Satyavati desired to have her as a granddaughter-in-law. Bheeshma had therefore gone and presented the marriage proposal on the queen mother's behalf, and had brought Madree to Hastinapur. Pandu was spending his life quite happily with his two wives. Kunti had three sons – Yudhishthir, Bheem and Arjun. Madree too had two sons – Nakul and Sahadeo. Thus Pandu had, with blessing of deities, five brave and virtuous sons – these were the Pandavs.

Dhritarashtra and Gaandhari had hundred sons. They were called Kouravs after the name of the dynasty Kuru. The family of the Kurus was thus flourishing.

But during a spring season, Pandu died suddenly. Handing over her sons Nakul and Sahadeo to Kunti, Madree preferred to die on the funeral pyre of Pandu. Satyavati, Ambika and Ambalika were quite grieved. The three went to the forest and spent the rest of their lives there in spiritual pursuits.

|| The Rise of Jealousy ||

The five Pandavs, and the hundred Kouravs grew
together. Among them, Bheem was the mightiest. No other
child could compete with him, at play or in fighting. Bheem was
particularly fond of trouncing, and trampling upon his cousins, the
Kouravs. He would indulge in all sorts of pranks and pester them. All
Kouravs, and Duryodhan in particular, were mortally afraid as also
angry with Bheem. 'How to tackle Bheem', was their concern all the
time.

Once Duryodhan and his brother Dusshaasan hatched a plot to
finish Bheem off. Through King Dhritarashtra, they got constructed
a playhouse on the banks of the Ganga at a place called Pramankoti.
It was kept well-stocked with abundant eatables. They proposed a
trip to that place along with the Pandavs. All of them went to the
place and played to their heart's content. Bheem, at the sight of the
river, jumped into the Ganga and swam heartily.

After quite a while, Duryodhan suggested,

"Come, let us eat. We are all quite hungry."

"Yes, let us go quickly," Bheem agreed.

All of them sat together for meals. Duryodhan was making a
great show of merriment, and was plying everybody with the food.
He was even feeding some with his own hands. During the meal,
Duryodhan picked up a handful and fed it to Bheem with the words,
"You must really be quite tired by swimming. Here, have this from
my hands!"

No sooner than the meals were over, than Bheem's eyes started
drooping – he had never felt drowsier. It was natural – Duryodhan
had mixed poison in the handful of food that he had fed to Bheem.

When he could no longer control his sleep, Bheem went to the
bank of the river and slept there. The other Pandavs were also

exhausted by the day's play; thus all of them went to sleep. Duryodhan grabbed the opportunity and tied up the sound asleep Bheem with wild creepers and rolled him over in the stream of the Ganga.

Come morning, and everyone arose and was ready to return to Hastinapur. But where was Bheem? A search started, but there was no sign of him. Afterwards, thinking that he might have proceeded on his own early in the morning, they all returned to Hastinapur. The wicked minds of Duryodhan and Dusshaasan were rejoicing. But the absence of Bheem made Kunti's heart tremble with fear. Her anxious mind feared the worst. The rest of the Pandavs were also equally worried.

‖ Bheem in the Naag country ‖

Bheem fell unconscious with the imbibed poison. When Duryodhan dumped his body in the river, he went straight to the bottom. On the riverbed lived many poisonous snakes. As many of them came under his rolling body, the snakes were crushed to death. Quite a few serpents bit Bheem in anger at many places. But wonder of wonders, the rock-like body of Bheem was not affected by their poison. On the contrary, their stings acted as an antidote against the poison he had been fed. He started to regain consciousness. The movements of his massive body and his terrible groans sent the whole Naag country into panic. The serpents started creeping to their King Vasuki in fear. Seeing them panic, Vasuki asked, "What is the matter? Do not panic!"

"The Naaglok has been invaded by a menace, my Lord!"

"What menace?"

Then the serpents narrated the story to Vasuki. Even Vasuki was surprised to hear of such a body and hastily approached Bheem. He asked Bheem, "Who are you?"

When he replied that he was Bheem, son of Kunti, Vasuki was pleased to hear it because Kunti's father was a grandson of the Naag Aryak, and thus Bheem came to be related to Naags. Vasuki felt that the newcomer was not a threat but a guest and embraced Bheem in welcome. He then proffered to Bheem, vats of a special juice, each packed with the power of a thousand Naags. Bheem managed to drink eight such vats of juice.

The following day, Vasuki felicitated Bheem and bade him a fond farewell. His serpent attendants then fetched Bheem up to the bank of the Ganga. Thus endowed afresh with extraordinary power, Bheem returned to Hastinapur. Seeing him come back safely, Kunti and Vidur were freed of their anxiety and both heaved a sigh of relief.

Drawing him closer, Kunti asked, "Where were you all this while, Bheem?"

"I visited the Naag country down under, mother," replied Bheem and gave her an account of what had befallen him. Then tightly clenching his fists, he declared,

"I will just go like this and teach that devil Duryodhan a thing or two–"

But Vidur made him tarry awhile. He said patiently,

"Wait for the right time, Bheem. You should wait till then. A wise man should not pay so much attention to the evil ones."

Yudhishthir, too, said, "Peace is the real ornament of the brave, Bheem, have you not heard this saying?"

" I'll be quiet," assumed Bheem and kept silent.

Thus Duryodhan's crafty moves brought in bitterness and it was the beginning of the sour Kourav-Pandav relationship, which turned into enmity.

|| Towards Learning ||

One day, the Kouravs and the Pandavs were playing on a ground. Their game was in full swing when the cloth ball they were playing with, flew off and fell into a well. The well was old, unused and deep. It was getting dark. It was not possible for them to take out the ball. They all stood around the well in gloom. A veteran Brahmin sage was passing by. Seeing the boys stand thus, he inquired, "What is wrong, boys?"

"We have lost our ball in the well, and we do not know how to fetch it."

"Whose children are you all?"

Yudhishthir came forth at this juncture, and told him the names of their ancestors with pride, beginning with Dushyant-Bharat right up to *pitamaha* Bheeshma. After hearing the list, the old Brahmin commented,

"Born in such a high family, and yet you cannot recover the ball from the well! Let me show you what trick good Kshatriya boys would use here."

And taking down the bow from his shoulder, he sent off an arrow. It went straight to the ball at the bottom. Another arrow that he sent off hit the tail of the first one. The third one hit the second, and so on up to the sixth. The tail of the sixth arrow came up to the rim of the well. The old sage then pulled out the arrows by grabbing it – and lo! The ball stuck at the tip of the first arrow also came out. The boys were glad and ran to grandfather Bheeshma to tell him the story. He immediately realized the archery skills of the Brahmin. An appreciator of virtue that Bheeshma was, he got up and went to the old Brahmin. But by then the old man was on his way. Catching up with him, Bheeshma greeted him and asked, "Are you the one who got the ball out of the well for my grandchildren?"

"Yes, my Lord. But if you have come with a wish to 'remunerate' me for such a simple task, leave it. I tell you. Not only shall I not accept anything, but I will feel it as a personal insult." Upon this, Bheeshma folded his hands to the Brahmin and said, "I do not presume to offer you anything, but wish to seek something from you humbly."

"What is that ?"

"I recognize you, my Lord. You are the well-known archer Drona. I wish that you take up as a teacher for the children. My grandchildren cannot hope to get a better teacher than you. Please accept my request."

When Bheeshma was requesting himself, it was not possible for Drona to refuse. He agreed to impart training to the Kouravs and the Pandavs. But Drona put down a condition. He said, "I want my *Guru-dakshina** but not in cash or any other valuables."

"What is your wish, then?"

"Let Drupad be defeated by my disciples. That would be my *dakshina.*"

"Why do you hate Drupad, teacher?" asked Bheeshma.

Dronacharya replied, "Drupad and myself were pupils at my father's ashram. We were classmates. Drupad used to tell me, 'Drona, my kingdom is your kingdom too'. Later on, he succeeded his father to the throne, and I continued as a teacher. That this calling is ill-paying and keeps one in poverty is well-known. My state was no different – so much that I could not even afford milk for my son, Ashvatthaama.

"Other children would drink milk and our son, too, would come to his mother and insist on having milk. She would, poor dear, make 'milk' by mixing flour in water. Ashvatthaama used to drink it with relish. But soon he learnt the taste of real milk and was quite mad at his mother. He came charging at her, crying 'You cheated me'. Finally it was decided that I should go to Drupad and get a cow from him.

"One day I went there and just began to talk to him by addressing him as 'Friend'. But Drupad, power-drunk and wealth-crazy, cut me short and said, 'You dumb fellow! A poor lacklustre beggar can never be a friend of a king like me!' I was shattered at these words as I expected friendship. Thus I want these pupils to teach a lesson to the rude, power-blind Drupad."

"I have entrusted these children to you. You may shape them into anything desirable," Bheeshma told him.

Dronacharya taught the Kouravs and the Pandavs archery, horse riding, fencing, chariot driving and mace fighting etc. In the last named activity Bheem and Duryodhan gained proficiency, and Nakul and Sahadeo in fencing. Arjun became a famous archer. In addition, he learnt various missiles and weapon specialities.

|| Karna Humiliated ||

Along with the Kouravs and the Pandavs, Drona's son, Ashvatthaama, as well as Karna, the son of Radha, were the pupils of Dronacharya. The infant that Kunti had abandoned in a basket to the mercy of the river had come in the hands of a servant in the stables of the Kouravs. The servant, a *soota* or a chariot driver by profession, had taken the baby home. His wife Radha nurtured the child as if it were her own. This child was Karna, also known as Radheya (son of Radha), who was as proficient as Arjun in the art of wielding weapons and missiles.

At the end of the training, Drona had arranged a test for his students. A sparrow made of clay was hung down a tree branch by a thread. The test included shooting an arrow through the eye of the sparrow.

Everyone now set an arrow to the bow. But before they began shooting, Drona asked everyone, "What do you see there?" Someone uttered the branch; others mentioned the leaves; a few others the sky. Some others mentioned 'only the sparrow'. Arjun replied, "Only the eye of the sparrow."

"Good! This is what concentration means. Go ahead, and shoot," directed Drona.

Arjun shot the arrow and it hit the sparrow right in the eye, breaking the bird into pieces. Arjun was praised by all.

The test was followed by a demonstration of the weapons proficiency of the Kouravs and the Pandavs in the presence of citizens of Hastinapur. Each prince came forth, and showed his particular skills – Arjun excelled in all of them. All those present praised him, and Arjun was all smiles, riding the crest of admiration. At this juncture, Karna came forth and said, "Wait, Arjun! I can show that I can also perform all that done by you."

"Bravo! That is the spirit, " cheered Duryodhan who was peeved at Arjun's glory. He encouraged Karna to compete with Arjun. Karna was, after all, his friend, and always used to move among the Kouravs. Karna challenged Arjun for a duel, as was customary for brave warriors. Bheem intervened,

"Of course, Arjun will take up the challenge. But the participants in a duel need to know each other's pedigree, family etc. Arjun is a prince from the Kuru family; but what about you? Do you know which family you come from?"

At this question, Karna had to look down with shame. What family shall he say he came from? Duryodhan saw his plight and announced, " From this very moment, Karna is the King of the Anga-desh!" and he put the crown of Anga-desh on Karna's head asking Bheem, "Is it all right now to fight the duel ?"

On this, Bheem said mockingly, "You may well make him the king with your charity, but he shall continue to be a *sootaputra* – son of a lowly chariot driver!"

Since a *soota* had brought up Karna, Bheem dared to call him in this fashion. Karna was really chagrined at this word and took it as a great insult. In fact, there was quite a fracas between the Kouravs and the Pandavs. But at about this time, the Sun was setting. Drona adroitly caught this opportunity to declare the tournament as concluded, due to sunset. A fight was avoided and everyone went home.

|| Guru-dakshina ||

After a few days, Drona said to the Kourav- Pandavs, "Brave princes! Your training is now over. It is time you paid me my *Guru-dakshina*. I hope, you have not forgotten about it."

"Never, O Guru. You only have to give a command, and we shall march against the Panchal country, and capture King Drupad," assured Duryodhan.

Arjun, Bheem, Karna were all ready. Drona set out taking the army of Kurus. First, it was the Kouravs to attack the Panchals, Drona remaining behind with the Pandavs. Drupad also had a ready massive army and he entered the fight to finish. He made a short work of Duryodhan, Dusshaasan and Karna within no time. Seeing the rout of the Kouravs, Drona ordered Arjun to the fore. Fighting bravely, Arjun pitted his chariot against that of Drupad and disarmed the enemy. Drupad was now helpless as, in the meantime, Bheem had polished off most of his army. Thus captured, the king was brought in shackles by the Pandavs to their Guru Drona. They said, "Here is your *Guru-dakshina*, Lord."

Drona congratulated them with a beaming smile.

He then turned to Drupad and asked,

"Do you recognize me? But how can you know a poor mendicant, as you are a king! "

Drupad stood with his head bowed in shame owing to the defeat. Drona then asked him,

"Your kingdom is now mine, Drupad; and I am the king here. What do you wish now as a prisoner before the king?"

"Drona, I admit I have ill-treated you under the influence of the power. You are now free to avenge as you wish," King Drupad replied in humility.

"I only wish to be called a friend of yours, Drupad," replied Drona.

"Friend Drona! I shall be happy and proud to claim your friendship again," Drupad said.

"I shall restore half of your kingdom to you, and the other half shall remain with me, friend. Please relieve my friend from the shackles, Arjun!" Drona ordered.

Drupad returned to his city with a heavy tread.

‖ The Flare up at Lakshagrih ‖

Due to the latest victory of the Pandavs, the Kouravs, particularly Duryodhan and Dusshaasan, started feeling quite jealous. Around this time, Bheeshma also declared Yudhishthir as the crown prince. As a result, the kingdom of Hastinapur was to go to the Pandavs. Finding them powerless, the Kouravs felt a nagging pain. Dhritarashtra was also drawn by an extraordinary love for his sons, and wished that they should succeed him on the throne. He plotted a plan with a minister called Kanik. Kanik was a past master of evil conspiracies. He suggested that the Pandavs, along with their mother Kunti, be sent to a place called Varnavat and asked to stay at the 'Lakshagrih' there.

Duryodhan readily approved of the plan. Dhritarashtra called Yudhishthir and said, "Why do not you brothers, along with mother Kunti, go for some rest and recreation to Varnavat? I feel, you should. In fact, I am getting a palace constructed there just for this purpose. Do live there happily, enjoy!"

Yudhishthir honoured the wishes of the elders and set out for Varnavat on an auspicious occasion.

Vidur was by relation an uncle of the Kuru princes. He was known to be quite a balanced, moral and religious person. The Pandavs treated Vidur with great respect, and since the Pandavs were themselves polite, Vidur was more inclined towards them than their cousins. Vidur hardly liked the machinations of the Kouravs.

Vidur sensed something amiss in the plan to send the Pandavs to Varnavat, and was, naturally, quite anxious. He then found out all about Varnavat from the secret agents. He was shocked when he learnt that the palace constructed for the Pandavs was made out of *lac,* a kind of raisin which contained highly inflammable materials such as gunpowder. With great alertness, Vidur managed to persuade one of the artisans working there and through him, got constructed an underground escape tunnel from that palace called Lakshagrih.

With the pretext of seeing off the Pandavs on their tour, Vidur travelled some distance with them. When at a safe distance from the capital, he warned Yudhishthir about the sinister motive in sending them off to Varnavat. He briefed the young prince about the secret of the Lakshagrih and also explained to him the escape route he had got constructed in the form of the tunnel. Having done the needful, he then retreated to the capital, after words of best wishes for their safety.

On reaching Varnavat, the Pandavs were led to the Lakshagrih by the servants. At least superficially, the servants appeared to be courteous to the Pandavs. The Pandavs spent the day there quite well. They also skilfully and secretly marked where the secret route to the tunnel began. At nightfall, they just got up and began walking down the tunnel. While leaving the surrounding area of the palace, Bheem threw back a flare and lit up the Lakshagrih. In no time there was a blinding flash, and the palace was on fire to get burnt down to cinders.

Finding a heap of ashes in place of the palace, Duryodhan was quite happy. He was under the impression that the Pandavs and Kunti were also burnt the previous night itself, making his way to the throne free.

The Pandavs however safely crossed the tunnel along with Kunti and reached the deep forest.

‖ Killing of Hidimb and Bakasoor ‖

Though a queen mother, Kunti now had to live in the woods; as the Pandavs along with their mother now lived only by taking refuge in the jungle. During such wanderings, once they had camped at a place where the demon Hidimb lived close by. Cruel and inhuman by nature, the hefty rakshasas (demons) were often cannibals. After sighting Kunti and the Pandavs, Hidimb's mouth watered with lust.

Hidimb sent his younger sister, Hidimba, to kill the Pandavs. Hidimba, though female, was equally fierce in her looks. When she approached the camp, Bheem was guarding the place. By finding herself among humans someone huge and at the same time quite handsome, Hidimba lost her heart to Bheem. Instead of killing them, she implored Bheem to somehow get away and escape from her brother's clutches.

Around then, Hidimb himself came there. Seeing Bheem, he attacked him, screaming fiercely. But with his unmatched power, Bheem lifted Hidimb high up in the air, dashed him against the ground over and over again, killing him. Hidimba then married Bheem and they had a son called Ghatotkach.

Further during their wanderings, the Pandavs went to a town called Ekachakra. They stayed at the house of a Brahmin. They found that the host was unhappy, deep down in gloom. Kunti asked him the reason. She learnt that the city-dwellers had to provide a cartful of food, and also a man, every day as food to a demon called Bakasoor. This practice had been going on by rotation and each household had to supply food and a person without fail. That day it was the turn of the Brahmin family, and their young son was to be sacrificed for the demon's hunger – that was why the family was grieving. Hearing this story Kunti too, felt sad, and she comforted the family.

Narrating the story to Bheem, Kunti said, "You ought to tackle this unjust demon Bakasoor."

Bheem was more than willing for such a task. The next day, Bheem, in place of the Brahmin son, rode on the cart of the food that went to Bakasoor. En route to the demon's place, Bheem polished off some food from the cart. On reaching the place, he also began gobbling the food from the cart right in front of the demon. Bakasoor was already enraged with acute hunger and was keenly waiting for the cart of food. Seeing Bheem's actions, his anger knew no bounds! He pounced on Bheem and started pummeling him left and right. But Bheem did not budge at all – he stayed put and quietly finished off all the food. Then giving out a loud burp, he roared,

"Now let me see what problem is there with you!"

And indeed, he felled Bakasoor down, sat on his chest and clobbered him to pulp.

At the death of Bakasoor, the people of Ekachakra were quite happy and they blessed Bheem, grateful for the brave rescue that Bheem had effected.

|| Droupadi's Svayamvar ||

Pandavs stayed at Ekachakra for some more days. Their host, the Brahmin, was quite pleased with them and imparted them training in *Ved-vidya*. One day Bhagwan Vedvyas arrived there and told them, "You should go to the Panchal country, sons. There Droupadi, the king's daughter from a yagna, is to marry in a *svayamvar*. You must take part in it; for there is a prophecy that Droupadi is born for the downfall of the Kouravs."

"Then we must all go there," said Arjun. The five Pandavs disguised as Brahmins set out along with their mother towards the Panchal country.

At nightfall, they camped near a lake. Gandharvs came here each night to frolic and play in the lake. When they saw the Pandavs there that night, they were angry. The Gandharv Angarparna showered arrows on the Pandavs. But Arjun blocked them all, and in reply launched the Agni missile. The missile burnt off the chariot of the Gandharvs and they surrendered to the Pandavs. Kunti however asked Arjun to let the Gandharvs go; and in gratitude for this release, one of them gave Arjun a special power: Chaakshushi. With it, anything happening anywhere in all three worlds could be seen sitting at one place. He also showed them the way to Dhoumya's ashram as per their desire.

Sage Dhoumya welcomed the Pandavs and asked what they wished. Yudhishthir said, "We wish that you should accept the position of the family priest with us." Dhoumya was quite glad to become their priest, and accompanied them to the Panchal capital for the *svayamvar*.

The proposed ceremony had brought kings and princes from various countries there. Among them were the Yadavs, Krishna and also Balram. Preparations for the *svayamvar* were quite elaborate. There was the customary *pana** : a pillar had been erected, on top of which was fitted a revolving fish. At the foot of the pillar was a large

.

pan full of oil, reflecting the revolving fish. The contestant had to shoot an arrow looking only at the reflection, to hit the eye of the fish. Only the one who could achieve this feat could marry Droupadi.

Many kings and princes from the assembly tried to shoot at the fish, but none of them was successful. Among those who had to go back disappointed were Duryodhan, Jayadrath, Shakuni. Seeing them fail, Karna rose and started readying his bow by setting the chord. Just then Droupadi announced, "I shall not marry a *sootaputra!*"

Thus snubbed, Karna had to sit down.

Then from the assembled Brahmins came forth Arjun. Bowing to the elders, he set his bow and within a flash of an eyelid, he had pierced the eye of the revolving fish. All those assembled were astonished at this never-seen-before skill in archery. Everyone wondered,

"Who could this brave Brahmin archer be?" But then shortly, they came to learn that he was Arjun.

The Pandavs are alive, after all! Their well-wishers and Droupadi herself were glad to hear this news, but the Kouravs, particularly Duryodhan, were quite peeved at the news.

The Pandavs along with Droupadi happily returned to their residence. Before entering their house, Yudhishthir called out, "We are victorious, mother! We have come with a priceless gem."

On hearing this, Kunti said from within, "Well done, you all five brothers share it!" Only after she came out, she realized that he was referring to Droupadi, a gem among women! But she had spoken already, and now her word had to be abided.

Those days, the custom of one woman marrying more than one man was prevalent in some parts of the country. Accordingly, Droupadi became the wife of the Pandavs.

|| Indraprastha ||

The conspiracy of Lakshagrih was foiled, the Pandavs were alive and they had even added to their glory by winning Droupadi. This was enough to set the evil mind of Duryodhan on fire. He was quite upset, and his father, Dhritarashtra, too was equally restless. But right-thinking men such as Bheeshma, Drona and Vidur prevailed upon him. They told the king, "Better invite the Pandavs to Hastinapur and give them half the kingdom honourably. It is wise and just. It is their right, and Krishna is their friend. It is impossible to defeat the Pandavs or destroy them – trying to do so, you will destroy yourself."

Duryodhan did not like this talk at all. Yet, Dhritarashtra, though not willing, consented to the suggestion. He entrusted to Vidur the responsibility of fetching the Pandavs to Hastinapur honourably.

Vidur came to the Pandavs, carrying rich ornaments, garments, the royal chariot and abundant wealth. Both were quite happy, meeting each other after a long time. After exchanging initial courtesies, Vidur told them the purpose of his visit. Yudhishthir decided to go to Hastinapur after consulting Shrikrishna, Kunti and father-in-law Drupad. Accordingly, the Pandavs came to Hastinapur along with Kunti and Droupadi.

Dhritarashtra appeared happy. Showing his pleasure, at least for the sake of show, he said, "I am glad you are safe, Yudhishthir. Now I offer you half the kingdom – you should accept it and live at Khandavprastha, I feel."

"Just as you wish, elder," said Yudhishthir.

Actually, Khandavprastha was an insignificant region with only jungle all around. It was the habitat of wild beasts. Shrikrishna and Arjun decided to create paradise out of this wilderness. They had the land levelled after burning the woods. Then Maharshi Vedvyas and other sages came and earmarked the land for the palace, as per religious precepts, after performing the necessary rites and chanting for *shanti**.

The work of erecting the capital began in right earnest. Architects, artists, painters, sculptors, supervisors – all trained professionals came together and created a magnificent city. Houses and gardens, roads and tanks, playgrounds and arbours, schools and auditoria, studios and theatres – the city had everything. Traders and professionals converged upon the city from near and far; and set up their shops and trades there. There was a strong fortification and a deep wide moat around the city. The watch towers known as *shataghnees* of the ramparts had cannons capable of killing hundreds. Thus the city was well-protected and wore a new dazzling look.

The Pandavs entered the city on an auspicious occasion with much fanfare. Yudhishthir named the new city Indraprastha.

The Pandavs now ruled their kingdom from Indraprastha.

|| Exile of Arjun ||

Since the Pandavs had married Droupadi, Sage Narad had laid down a rule for them, that no Pandav shall enter the room where any other brother was meeting Droupadi alone. If anyone broke this rule, he was to go away on an exile for twelve years. All Pandavs had agreed to abide by this decision.

One day Arjun was in dilemma. Some miscreants were forcibly taking away the cows of a poor Brahmin. Threatened by them, the Brahmin had come to Arjun and requested that he should save him from the marauders and protect the cows.

Arjun assured the poor Brahmin that there was no need to panic, and went in the armoury to get his weapons. But the way to the armoury lay through the room where Yudhishthir and Droupadi were resting. Arjun had no other course but to disturb them. He quickly gathered his arrows and bow; and went after the thieves. In no time, he managed to release the cows of the poor Brahmin.

Immediately on return, he came to Yudhishthir and confessed that he had made the mistake of breaking the rule set by Sage Narad. Yudhishthir tried to convince him, insisting that no wrong was done; Arjun was only acting in the interest of the *praja**, which was after all his duty.

But Arjun did not consider this concession offered by his elder brother. He insisted upon undergoing the exile as prescribed, dressed himself as a poor Brahmin, and took to the woods, to serve the term of the Narad-prescribed punishment.

Arjun used the period of exile to visit various shrines and religious places. He enjoyed the beauty of Nature throughout his journey; and took this opportunity to call on various sages and to discuss with them matters of higher wisdom.

As he travelled far and wide, he reached the Naag country. There

Uloopi, the daughter of the Naag king Kauravya, was quite overwhelmed by love at the first sight of Arjun. Arjun reciprocated and married Uloopi.

Travelling afterwards, through the Kalinga country Arjun reached Manipur, which was the seaside capital city. King Chitravaahan ruled there, and here Chitraangada, the daughter of the king, became the focus of Arjun's attraction. Arjun was so much in love with the princess that he approached the King Chitravaahan and sought the hand of the princess in marriage. Arjun was an eligible groom and as per the custom prevailing then, the king married off Chitraangada to the prince-charming of the Pandavs. In the course of time, Chitraangada gave birth to a son who was named Babhruvaahan. He later became the King of Manipur.

Arjun's further travels took him to Prabhas-teerth (a shrine in modern day Gujarat). Here he met Shrikrishna. As to a good friend, Arjun told him of all the happenings of his exile till then. Taking Arjun with him, Shrikrishna later went to Dwaraka. On the way was Mount Raivatak.

Here, a mountain festival was going on, and people of Dwaraka were visiting Raivatak in their finest clothes and ornaments. The mountain itself was well decked up. In such an atmosphere, Arjun was mingling with the men and women of Dwaraka, enjoying their festivities. And then Shrikrishna's sister Subhadra and Arjun met and fell in love. However, Shrikrishna's elder brother Balram had already decided to marry sister Subhadra to King Duryodhan. Balram, a headstrong person, was not likely to listen to any appeal in this regard. Shrikrishna himself, managed things in such a way that Arjun could elope with Subhadra.

In those days, elopement and marrying was a recognized form of marriage, particularly among the Kshatriyas and the royals. Later on, a marriage ceremony took place formally where Arjun and Subhadra received blessings from the elders. Subhadra gave birth to a brilliant son from Arjun and he was named Abhimanyu.

Droupadi had five sons from the five Pandav brothers. The son of Yudhishthir was Prativindhya, Bheem's son was Sutsom. Arjun's son was Shrutkarma, Nakul's Shataanik and Sahadeo's son was Shrutsen. Along with these five brothers, Abhimanyu also received training in the art of weaponry and they all became brave and expert warriors like their fathers.

After Arjun's exile was over, one day, as he was sitting with Shrikrishna at Indraprastha, Lord Agni came there *incognito**. He was disguised as a poor Brahmin and sought from them the Khandav-van forest. Shrikrishna and Arjun recognized Lord Agni and pleased him by giving him the forest as desired. On this occasion, Agni gave the famous Gandeev bow to Arjun along with a quiver of arrows that never ran out of stock. The chariot, with the ensign of monkey-god fluttering atop, was also gifted by Agni. Shrikrishna too received his special weapon *Sudarshan-chakra* from Agni at this juncture.

|| *Yudhishthir Performs Rajsooya* ||

Twelve years had passed since the establishment of the capital at Indraprastha. Yudhishthir, with the help of his brothers, had expanded their kingdom considerably, and the Pandavs now were an important dynasty in north India. Their subjects were happy, the coffers of the kingdom were also full. Yudhishthir felt that the time was ripe to perform the Rajsooya yagna.

Just around then, Sage Narad visited Indraprastha. When Yudhishthir expressed his wish to the sage, he seconded it, and asked him to consult Shrikrishna about the possible hurdles in the path. Shrikrishna then told Yudhishthir that it was impossible to have a smooth yagna until Jarasandh, the ruler of Magadh, was subdued. Yudhishthir naturally wanted to know about this task from him. Shrikrishna explained to him how to tackle Jarasandh.

Jarasandh was a powerful king. His army was quite large, and his influence had spread quite wide. He had thrown many neighbouring kings in the dungeon, and had not spared even the women of these royal houses from imprisonment. Insulting the righteous was his favourite pastime. To fight a war against such a powerful tyrant meant inviting major destruction.

Shrikrishna therefore advised,

"Jarasandh is a mighty proud wrestler and always rises to a challenge gladly. Let us challenge him for a bout of wrestling and finish him. Bheem is quite appropriate for this task."

Accordingly, Arjun, Bheem and Shrikrishna himself, dressed up as Brahmins and approached Jarasandh. They challenged him to fight a wrestling bout with any one of them.

A brave man seldom turns down a challenge, and, if a duel is to be fought, it is with a fighter suitable to his stature. Thus Jarasandh chose to fight with Bheem from among the three.

The fight continued for fourteen long days and yet there was no end in sight. On the fourteenth day, noting that Jarasandh was a little slack in his grasp, Shrikrishna signalled Bheem to try a different hold. Accordingly, Bheem lifted the mighty Jarasandh in the air, and threw him down with a bang. He then sat on his chest and hit Jarasandh with all might so hard that Jarasandh died there and then!

By then the Pandav army reached the border of Magadh. With the death of Jarasandh, the Magadh kingdom was brought under the Pandav empire. All the kings, their womenfolk and other unlucky good people who were in the Magadh prisons were freed by the Pandavs. All of them and the oppressed subjects of Magadh blessed the Pandavs and shouted slogans wishing them all success. Arjun, Bheem and Shrikrishna returned to Indraprastha, having entrusted the throne of Magadh to Sahadev, the son of Jarasandh.

Once it was decided to perform the Rajsooya yagna, Arjun, Bheem, Nakul and Sahadeo went in all four directions in order to get the plentiful funds needed for it, and to ensure allegiance of the kings. They conquered all that they encountered on route and brought home vast quantities of wealth.

As preparations for the yagna were being done, invitations for the ceremony were sent out to various sages, ascetics, neighbouring kings, seniors and well-wishers all around. All honoured the invitation and came to the yagna. Among those gracing the pandal were the elders such as *pitamaha* Bheeshma, Dronacharya, Vidur and even Kouravs led by Duryodhan and Dusshaasan from Hastinapur.

Yudhishthir welcomed them all and had made appropriate provisions of hospitality for their sake. Besides, considering their close relationship, responsibilities such as safekeeping the funds, catering in the pandal were delegated to Duryodhan and Dusshaasan, respectively. Bheeshma and Dronacharya supervised the arrangements personally. Lord Krishna, however, had, humbly chosen the task of clearing the plates after guests had eaten the banquet.

The rites of yagna were over, and the time came for offering the ceremonial worship, *arghya** in gratitude, to the most deserving person. Yudhishthir sought the counsel of *pitamaha* Bheeshma as to who should be chosen for this honour. The elder said, "The person

most venerable, and having all virtues deserving to receive the *arghya* here is none but Shrikrishna. He should be the one to receive the offering first."

Everyone, including the seniors in the pandal, agreed.

Yudhishthir and the other Pandavs were overjoyed by this verdict.

There was one jarring note, though. Shishupal, King of Chedi, was quite angry at this decision. He got up and began censuring Shrikrishna, Yudhishthir, Bheem and others using the foul language. The seniors tried to reason with him but Shishupal was adamant and rude.

Shrikrishna thereupon said, "Shishupal has now crossed the limit of a hundred evil deeds. I had promised his mother, who is my aunt that I shall not act until Shishupal commits a hundred evil deeds. I have kept the promise so far. Now that he has troubled the entire Yadav community so much, there is no other way but to punish him." Thus saying, he sent out his *Sudarshan- chakra* and beheaded Shishupal. Barring this one incident, the Rajsooya was a grand success.

Maharshi Vedvyas however struck a note of caution and said, "Much impressed and happy as I am seeing your success and wealth, remember well, that success of one is invariably the cause of envy in the minds of the other in the family. Though you are a honour to your family, such envy often leads to hatred and one-upmanship that cause the final fall. Even as you are engaged in rising above, see to it that you do not deviate from truth and that unnecessary bloodshed is avoided."

‖ The Game of Dice ‖

Maya was a great architect. When he was running for life from the flames of the fire in Khandav-van, Arjun had saved him. In gratitude, Maya had constructed a special hall at Indraprastha for Yudhishthir. It was named after the architect as Mayasabha. Not only was its beauty unsurpassed, it was full of many miracles. For instance, its crystal floor looked like water; and on the other hand where one thought there was water, lay hard floor. This had misled even Duryodhan.

After the Rajsooya yagna, Duryodhan, along with his maternal uncle Shakuni, stayed over at Indraprastha. One day, he was going around with Droupadi and the Pandavs to have a look at the Mayasabha. At one place, Duryodhan lifted up his garments and treaded cautiously, thinking that there was water ahead. But there was hard ground, no water. This gave rise to a laugh of ridicule from Bheem.

On the other hand, at another place Duryodhan went ahead confidently and found himself all wet through, having fallen in a pool of water which had seemed so much like plain ground to him. Here, Droupadi laughed at him. Further, as he was walking straight ahead thinking there was a door, he ran into a wall and crashed. Bheem laughed aloud and said, "After all, it is the blind son of a blind father!" Droupadi had been still laughing since the earlier occasion. Duryodhan felt quite humiliated. He kept mum at that time, but his pride was hurt.

The following day, returning to Hastinapur with Shakuni-*mama*, he was quite depressed and silent. Shakuni asked,

"What is the matter, Duryodhan? Why are you so glum?"

"Did you not see and hear what happened yesterday? Do you think it was pleasant? What a glorious life have these Pandavs created around them! How can we tolerate it meekly? No, *mama*, at least I cannot tolerate it," replied Duryodhan.

Shakuni agreed with Duryodhan.

"Do not merely agree with me. Tell me how I can strip the Pandavs of this glory. It does not seem possible to vanquish them in a war."

"No, no! Do not even think of a war."

"What then?" asked Duryodhan.

"We have to employ very subtle tricks," replied Shakuni. "Yudhishthir is quite fond of a game of dice, you know. Call him through your father to Hastinapur for a tournament of dice, and leave the rest to me."

Uncle Shakuni was a master in the art of cheating at dice. By nature also, he was crooked and wicked. Duryodhan also had the same feelings as Shakuni. He went to Dhritarashtra and insisted that he call the Pandavs for a game of dice. Dhritarashtra too was jealous of the prosperity of the Pandavs. He made a show of not wanting to drag the Pandavs in any such plan, and asked Vidur's advice.

Vidur openly opposed any such plan, and also warned that this plan was evil and would lead to a catastrophic situation and requested Dhritarashtra to desist. But Dhritarashtra was in no mood to listen to Vidur, largely due to Duryodhan's insistence. Just as he was physically blind, from within also he had become mentally blind owing to excessive love for his son. Leave alone listening to Vidur, he went on to advise him not to see evil in fun and games; this habit of seeing bad in everything is no good. He then sent an invitation to Yudhishthir for the game of dice.

On receipt of the invitation, the Pandavs also smelt a rat in the Kouravs' intention, just as Vidur had done. Droupadi, Bheem and Arjun expressed their opinion that the dice playing invitation should be declined. But Yudhishthir made much of the fact that the invitation had come from Dhritarashtra, and maintained that an elder's wish must be respected. Finally it was decided that all should go to Hastinapur.

The game of dice began. But as planned, Shakuni played like a cheat. Yudhishthir lost many a game. For each game he went on putting at stake all his wealth, the kingdom, his servants, his brothers, and finally himself. And he lost each of these games and stakes. Though he had lost all, the game was not yet over.

Finally he put Droupadi at stake, and that game also was won by Duryodhan. Thus all Pandav brothers, and also Droupadi, became slaves of the Kouravs. Droupadi was called out and Dusshaasan dragged her out by grabbing her hair in full view of the court. The evil Kourav did not even think it anything untoward to tug at her clothes to disrobe her. Finding all her five husbands incapable of protecting her, Droupadi prayed to Shrikrishna. Shrikrishna, in an invisible form, kept on providing her with unlimited length of clothing as Dusshaasan kept on dragging it. Thus she did not have to suffer further ignominy, and her honour was protected.

Reacting to this totally vile behaviour of the Kouravs, the saner elements from the Kourav's court such as Vidur left the hall. Seniors such as Bheeshma, Drona had to simply sit with bowed heads. However Gaandhari took pity on Droupadi's plight. She requested her husband to put a stop to this foul play forthwith. Dhritarashtra then reined in Duryodhan, and let the Pandavs go. Before leaving, Droupadi took a solemn vow: her hair, dishevelled by Dusshaasan, shall now be done up only by applying a coating of his blood.

Bheem who could barely control his anger and was sitting quiet so far, burst out at this, "I shall fulfill this vow of yours, Droupadi. What is more, the devil Duryodhan's thigh shall be shattered with my mace."

The Pandavs left, but their parting words were enough to shake Duryodhan. He was also angry with his parents as they had intervened and made him leave his plan midway. He had no appetite, and became leaner day by day like a sick man. Dhritarashtra was quite worried.

For the sake of his blind love for his son, he once again invited

Yudhishthir for another game of dice. Though aware of a possible foul play behind this fresh invitation, Yudhishthir decided to accept it as a senior's wish. Like his other name Dharma, he was too righteous a person to refuse even such an invitation.

During this visit, Shakuni said to him,

"Yudhishthir, there shall be only one game this time. But the condition shall be: if you lose, all you Pandavs are to leave the regal glory, wear tree-bark clothes and go on a 12-year exile, at the end of which you also shall have to remain *incognito* for a year. During this year, if the Kouravs find you out, you will undergo another exile of twelve years."

Yudhishthir agreed to play even with this condition. Once again the dice was cast and as ill-luck would have it, he lost.

The Pandavs set down all their regal finery. They took up garments made of tree-bark. Entrusting mother Kunti to Vidur, Droupadi and the Pandavs set out for the exile.

The Kouravs – Duryodhan, Dusshaasan – and their friends like Karna, Shakuni were overjoyed at this turn of fate that the Pandavs had to suffer.

‖ In Exile ‖

Pandavs being sent out on exile was a matter of great grief to their subjects. Many people willingly gave up their home, comforts, and set out to join the Pandavs in the travails of their forest stay. Yudhishthir somehow convinced them and made them go back. After hearing of the exile, friends and relatives of the Pandavs, even the neighbouring kings came to call on them in the forest. Yudhishthir was touched by this love expressed by all.

Among the visitors was Drishtadyumna, brother of Droupadi, and Shrikrishna who had specially come down from Dwaraka. His words of support uttered with love, gave much relief to the Pandavs and Droupadi. Drishtadyumna took with him his nephews, the sons of Droupadi, to the Panchal city. Shrikrishna also arranged to keep Subhadra and Abhimanyu with him during the period of exile. Only Droupadi insisted, "I want to suffer the travails of the exile with my husbands!"

The Pandavs subsequently shifted to the forest called Dvaitvan. They set up a little hut there and lived in it. They used to subsist on fruit, roots and tubers available in the forest.

Days passed without any event. One day as the Pandavs were sitting and having a chat, Droupadi said, "We must avenge the wrong done to us by the Kouravs."

Yudhishthir, true to his name Dharma, replied, "Forgiveness is the ornament of the brave. We ought to forgive even staunch enemies."

This answer did not satisfy Droupadi. Bheem was all the time raring to go on rampage against the injustice of the Kouravs. Just then Maharshi Vedvyas arrived. Upon listening to them all, he said, "Arjun should procure the divine weapons so that you can defeat the Kouravs. The deities have hidden their weapons with Indra due to their fear of the demon Vritrasoor. Arjun can obtain the weapons by virtue of penance."

Following the advice, Arjun proceeded to Mount Indraneel to perform penance. Seeing Arjun's rigorous penance, Indra came down and asked, "Why have you undertaken such a rigorous penance?"

Arjun made it known to him that he wanted to be successful in effecting a revenge against the devilish Kouravs who had forced him and his near and dear ones into exile.

Indra then advised him that he should win the favour of Lord Shankar. Arjun now began a fresh penance in the Himalayas. One day, he found that a huge wild boar was rushing at him, threatening him with its tusks. Arjun lost no time to shoot out an arrow at the boar. And almost simultaneously, a Kiraat (Bhil-like tribesman) also shot out an arrow at the boar. This Kiraat was none other than Lord Shankar, who had taken this guise with a view to test Arjun. An argument ensued between them as to whose catch the boar was. Matters led to a duel between the Kiraat and Arjun. After a furious battle, Lord Shankar was pleased at the bravery, skill as well as weaponry expertise of Arjun. He bequeathed the missile *Pashupat-astra** to Arjun.

Later, Arjun lived with Lord Indra for some time. He was a favourite of Indra and received some more missiles from him. Due to his extraordinary powers of seeing through the veil of time and space, Indra suggested that it was advisable for Arjun to learn music and dancing. Arjun acquired skills in both the arts from a Gandharv called Chitrasen.

The remaining Pandavs in the meanwhile undertook a pilgrimage of the entire country and visited all shrines along with the Sage Lomas. As they were passing Badri-Kedar, the breeze brought along the fragrance of a special variety of lotuses. Droupadi expressed the desire to have the flowers. Bheem therefore set out to fetch the flowers. He ran into the Lord of Strength, Maruti, on the way. After Bheem and Maruti had a word, Maruti agreed to ride as an ensign on the flag, for Arjun's chariot. He also showed Bheem the lake where those special lotuses grew.

This lake was near the Gandhmaadan mountain, and it was guarded by some fierce demons. Bheem fought with them and killed them. Hearing this, Kuber himself arrived there. He recognized Bheem and offered him all the lotuses in his lake.

|| 'We are a Hundred plus Five' ||

Duryodhan kept on thinking up schemes of further harassing and humiliating the Pandavs, though they were already undergoing the exile. He consulted Shakuni and Karna. Shakuni suggested that inspection of the cattle stables at the Dvaitvan could be a good pretext to go to that forest. Duryodhan made a proposal of such a visit to Dhritarashtra, and some Kouravs with their army descended upon the Dvaitvan. They had even brought their wives with them. The whole exercise was aimed at heaping more ignominy upon the Pandavs.

Around the same time by strange coincidence, the celestial being Chitrasen Gandharv also came to the lake in Dvaitvan and all the heavenly beings together with wives and companions were having fun and frolic in the lake. When Duryodhan set out towards the lake, he was barred from proceeding further. Angered by this action Duryodhan challenged the Gandharv for a fight. In their first flush of enthusiasm, Karna and Dusshaasan attacked the Gandharv with a small army contingent. But Chitrasen immediately made short work of them. Duryodhan mustered rest of the army and attacked him with a great show of strength. But Chitrasen fired the *Gandharv-astra*, which in one swoop tied up the whole Kourav army.

Duryodhan, Dusshaasan, Shakuni and all other Kourav warriors were in quite a pitiable state. Seeing the plight of their masters, a handful of Kourav soldiers somehow managed to escape the vigil of the Gandharvs and ran for life towards the forest where the Pandavs stayed. There, they approached Yudhishthir who was engaged in performing a yagna. The soldiers simply lay prostrate at his feet and said, "The honour of Kurus can now be saved only by you, my Lord! Karna has fled, and the enemy has tied up Duryodhan, Dusshaasan and all the Kouravs like cattle. The mighty Gandharv has not spared even the womenfolk from the Kourav entourage from this punishment of captivity."

As the incident was being narrated, Bheem was sitting nearby. Hearing the account of the plight of the Kouravs, he started laughing aloud. He said, "Well served! I am so glad that the Kouravs have been shown their place. Those who hurt others deserve to get such treatment themselves!"

While Bheem was pleased at the events, Dharmaraj was pained. He said to Bheem,

"My dear brother, they may be crooked, they may behave like enemies, but the Kouravs after all are our brethren. Can anybody, may he be from heaven, come and tie them up like cattle? That is not at all a matter of pride and laughter for us. What is their insult is an insult to us too. We must strive to maintain our family honour.

"When we fight among ourselves, the score may be 'Five *versus* Hundred'. But when it comes to a struggle with some outsider, we are a Hundred plus Five. Bear this well in mind, and we must show it to the enemy also.

"If I were not engaged in the yagna, I myself would have gone to fight with the Gandharv. But why worry, when all you brothers are quite capable of doing the needful. Bheem, go and show the Gandharv what prowess you have, and free our Kourav brethren."

As per the orders of the elder brother, Bheem, Arjun, Nakul and Sahadeo went at war with the Gandharv. Arjun's skill with *astra*s fixed the Gandharv for good. Looking at it, Chitrasen preferred to surrender. Then as asked by Arjun, he released Duryodhan, Dusshaasan and the womenfolk of the Kourav family. All Kouravs went away, their heads hanging low in shame.

|| The Test of Virtue ||

Duryodhan was quite unhappy that his friends and himself had to return in disgrace from their campaign to humiliate the Pandavs. But this only fuelled his hatred against them. Any good going their way was intolerable to him, and he kept looking for opportunities to bring them some harm.

One day, Sage Durvas along with a host of his disciples called on Duryodhan at his court. Duryodhan offered them all the tributes due to a great sage and his disciples; and hosted a lunch for them. Pleased, Durvas said, "You have succeeded in winning my favour, O Lord of Kurus. Ask me for whatever boon you desire."

Durvas was widely known for his volatile temperament. It would be proper to use this feature for troubling the Pandavs, felt Duryodhan and his friends Karna and Shakuni. As briefed by them, Duryodhan said to Durvas, "Maharshi, I wish that you should go to the Pandavs with all your disciples, and test their honour by unexpectedly seeking meals for you all."

"So be it!" agreed Durvas and called on the Pandavs deliberately way past the time of lunch, with a huge hoard of disciples with him. The Pandavs and Droupadi had finished their meals at that time and were sitting and chatting. When Durvas arrived, Yudhishthir offered him the customary welcome. Durvas said, "We shall go to the river, finish our ablutions and *sandhya**. In the meantime, prepare our meals."

Thus saying, Durvas proceeded to the river. It was just not possible for the Pandavs to possess the foodstuffs necessary for such a large group. Naturally, as provider and housewife, Droupadi was worried. She prayed to Shrikrishna. Answering her call, Shrikrishna appeared promptly and said, "Droupadi, I am very hungry. Please give me something to eat."

"Have you too come to test me, Krishna?" asked Droupadi. "You know how we live. There is not a grain of rice left at home for these guests, that is why I called you. See the plates; they are all washed up and are set aside for drying."

"Just see, there might be something there in the plate," said Shrikrishna. Droupadi brought him the plate which was washed and kept upside down to dry. There was just a little vegetable leaf sticking to the inside of the plate. Shrikrishna ate just that leaf with great relish and burped in satisfaction.

Shrikrishna had seen what Durvas was trying to do. As soon as he ate and burped, the sage and his disciples, who had just finished bathing at the river, started getting one burp after another, as if they had had a hearty meal. They were at a loss to know how this was happening. Their tummies were so full that they found it impossible to go to the Pandavs and eat anything there.

Therefore Durvas and his disciples abandoned all thoughts of a meal at the Pandavs' and found their way out of the forest right from the riverside itself.

Thus the honour of the Pandavs was preserved by Shrikrishna, and the grateful Pandavs were happy.

‖ Abduction of Droupadi ‖

The sting of ill will hurt Duryodhan all the more after his bid to humiliate the Pandavs through Durvas came to nothing. He was particularly peeved at Droupadi, and always looked for opportunities to disgrace her.

During this time, Jayadrath, brother-in-law of Duryodhan, was visiting him. Duryodhan mentioned to him that the twelve years of exile for Pandavs were about to end. Shortly, they would also finish the one-year period of *incognito* and shall come forth to claim their share of the kingdom, he feared. Therefore one must do away with them at the earliest. Jayadrath also shared with Duryodhan this feeling of hatred against the Pandavs. Besides, it was better for him if Duryodhan ruled, and not the Pandavs. Thus he said to Duryodhan,

"Let me go to the forest, find the Pandavs and do whatever I can."

Thus assuring Duryodhan, Jayadrath went to Dvaitvan. As he approached the ashram of the Pandavs, he found that all five Pandavs had gone in the deep forest for hunting, and Droupadi was all alone. Jayadrath barged into the ashram and sought to entice Droupadi by telling her how she would benefit by coming with him. He said,

"Come on, consent to come with me, and you can even be my favourite queen!"

Droupadi was livid with anger at this proposal. She retaliated, "Do not forget your status, Jayadrath. I am the wife of Pandavs – bear that well in your mind before you speak. Me, your Queen? Bah–"

Listening to this stinging rebuke from Droupadi, Jayadrath lost his temper. He simply grabbed Droupadi, and dumping her in his chariot, started driving it fast towards the city. Droupadi was screaming, and the screams were heard by the Pandavs returning from the forest.

Bheem and Arjun hurried and caught up with Jayadrath. As soon as he saw the two Pandavs, Jayadrath let Droupadi down from the chariot and tried to escape as fast as he could.

But Bheem caught him by the neck and tying him up, brought him before Yudhishthir. Droupadi shouted at him, "This villain dared to catch my hair and dragged me into his chariot. Off with those hands of his!"

Yudhishthir replied, "Jayadrath has certainly erred and is liable to be punished. But we cannot raise our hands to hit him for he is in our relation. He has married our cousin Duryodhan's sister. Therefore, we have to forgive him and let him go!"

At the elder's command, Bheem released Jayadrath.

Upon being released, Jayadrath's hatred for the Pandavs grew still more. He began a rigorous penance in the Himalayas with the purpose of defeating the Pandavs. Lord Shankar was pleased with his penance and granted him a boon that one day Jayadrath shall succeed in defeating all the Pandavs, except Arjun.

‖ Test of Yudhishthir's Integrity ‖

One day while the Pandavs were wandering through the forests, Yudhishthir felt thirsty, and sent Sahadeo to fetch water. Sahadeo immediately went to a nearby lake. He was himself thirsty. As he bent down to drink water, a voice called in a deep tone,

"Stop!"

Sahadeo was surprised. He looked hither and thither, and then asked, "Who is it who is stopping me?"

"I am a Yaksha*. The lake belongs to me. You can touch these waters only after you answer my questions."

Ignoring this instruction, Sahadeo took up a little water in his hands, and began to drink. He immediately fell unconscious.

'It has been quite some time since Sahadeo has gone, but he had not returned', wondered Yudhishthir and sent Nakul to check after him. But Nakul also met with the same fate. After this, Arjun and Bheem were also sent by Yudhishthir. But they too could not fare any better.

Since one after the other, four brave brothers had gone for a simple job, and had not returned, Yudhishthir himself came down to the lakeside. Finding Sahadeo, Nakul, Arjun and Bheem lying unconscious, he was shocked and pained too. He too bent down to take a little water, and heard the same deep voice calling,

"Wait!"

Surprised, Yudhishthir asked, "Why?"

"I am the Yaksha who owns this lake. Your brothers have met this fate because they tried to bypass me."

"What did they do to offend you?"

"They did not answer my questions. Anyone who does not reply my questions cannot touch the water."

"O Yaksha! You may ask me all your questions. I shall try to answer them to the best of my ability," said Yudhishthir.

The Yaksha asked,

"Which is the perennial religion?"

"Moksha *is the perennial religion.*"

"What gives you real recognition?"

"*Donating generously.*"

"What is the proper instrument of obtaining heaven and real pleasure?"

"*Truth and good character.*"

"Who is greater than the earth?"

"*The mother.*"

"Who is taller than the skies?"

"*The father.*"

"Who is faster than the wind?"

"*The mind.*"

"Which is the best instrument of gaining real wealth?"

"*A straight and cautious way of dealing.*"

"Which is the best wealth?"

"*Knowledge.*"

"What gain is the best gain?"

"*Health.*"

"Which pleasure is the best among all pleasures?"

"*Contentment.*"

"Which is the greatest religion?"

"*Compassion.*"

"With whom should one make friends so that the relation does not go wrong?"

"*The righteous.*"

"By leaving what does man win popularity with all?"

"*Pride.*"

"The forsaking of what leads to happiness?"

"Greed."

"Who is the real saint?"

"He, who strives for the welfare of all, always."

Thus the Yaksha went on asking all types of questions and Yudhishthir answered all the questions, to the complete satisfaction of the Yaksha. He was pleased with Yudhishthir. The Yaksha was, in fact, none other than Lord Yamadharma. Obtaining a boon from Yama, Yudhishthir restored his four brothers to consciousness. He also prayed for blessings from Yamadharma: now that their twelve years of exile were successfully completed, the one-year period of anonymity should also pass without any hitch.

Yamadharma granted him his wish and said,

"So be it!"

|| In Viraat's Country ||

Upon completing the 12-year period of their exile, the Pandavs had to spend the following year very cautiously. The Kouravs would leave no stone unturned to expose them during this year when they were supposed to remain *incognito*. According to the terms of the exile, if the Kouravs succeeded in finding out the Pandavs, the Pandavs would be required to serve another term of twelve years of exile.

At the end of the 12-year *vanvaas**, the Pandavs sat together and considered their plan seriously. As per the advice given earlier by Vidur, they decided that they would spend the year in the country ruled by King Viraat. One night, at the end of their exile, they came to the boundary of the capital of King Viraat's kingdom. They had come through the thickest of the forests, through the deep of valleys, taking all possible care not to be seen by anyone on the thoroughfares.

As things stood, due to the years of exile, they all had changed considerably in appearance. But Arjun's bow Gandeev and Bheem's mace would have surely made them stand out. They decided to conceal all their weapons in a graveyard on the outskirts of the city. They all set down their weapons, wrapped them securely and kept the bundle high up in a hollow on a Shami tree. As a measure of extra precaution, they also hung a corpse on that Shami tree.

Early morning the next day, each of them went to King Viraat's court, turn by turn in disguise. Yudhishthir had become a Brahmin priest. He went to Viraat and introduced himself as 'Kank'. He also told the king that he was well-versed in statecraft as well as the game of dice. On this basis Kank desired employment in Viraat's court, and the king too, gladly obliged.

A little later, Bheem arrived and introduced himself as a master-cook called Ballav who was conversant with the art of wrestling as well as that of cooking. As to his previous experience, he referred to Yudhishthir's name. When such a chef desired to work with him, King Viraat duly employed him.

After some time, it was Arjun. He called himself Brihannada and was dressed likewise in a woman's apparel. The study of song and dance completed at the advice of Indra was now going to be of good use to him in seeking employment. He was employed as an expert in dancing and singing, to teach his daughter, Uttara.

In a similar manner, Nakul came as horse-expert, Granthik and Sahadeo as a veterinarian called Tantipal; and they got employed in the court of King Viraat.

Droupadi came as Sairandhri and sought the position of a companion of Queen Sudeshna. She had served in a similar capacity with Krishna's consort Satyabhaama as also with Pandav empress Droupadi, she stated. She told the queen that the five Gandharvs were her husbands and they, in an invisible form, protected her all the while. Befitting her status, she laid down conditions such as she will not serve an alien male, nor will she wash anybody's feet; moreover, she was never to be given leftovers from anybody's plate as it would be polluted. The good queen Sudeshna agreed to the conditions and kept Sairandhri with her.

Thus the Pandavs with Droupadi, began the final year at the end of their long exile in the country of Viraat.

|| Slaying of Keechak ||

Yudhishthir, Bheem, Arjun, Nakul, Sahadeo and Droupadi, all were performing their roles well in the one-year period. Particularly, Kank with his competent attention towards governance, and Ballav with his skills in excellent cooking, had made King Viraat quite happy.

As days passed thus, time came for the festival of the local deity of the Viraat capital. It was the practice of the citizens of Viraat's capital, as well as the neighbouring settlements, to celebrate this festival with great fanfare. There would be a huge fair; and concerts of song, dance and drama would take place in it. There was also the tradition of having a massive bout of wrestling which attracted wrestlers from near and far.

That year the main attraction was a wrestler called Jeemoot. His fame was spread quite wide, as he had floored many well-known wrestlers. That year, he threw a challenge to come and fight with him. But with his formidable reputation, nobody came forward to take up the challenge. It upset King Viraat and he asked Ballav to go and fight with Jeemoot. As it is, Bheem was raring to go and show Jeemoot his prowess, since he was very well capable of finishing him off within no time. But he was holding himself back so that he should not be recognized as Bheem. He carefully kept fighting for a little while for the sake of appearances before defeating him. With this show of valour by Ballav, Viraat and his people also were happy.

Thus ten months of the year had passed. One day, as the king's brother-in-law Keechak, had come to call on his sister, Queen Sudeshna, he happened to see Sairandhri. Seeing such a beauty in his sister's palace was a pleasant surprise, and Keechak lusted for Sairandhri. He asked his sister Sudeshna to send Sairandhri for his service.

This request placed Queen Sudeshna in a dilemma. It was hard to turn down Keechak's request, as he was not just her brother, but a main warrior leading the Viraat army. The survival of Viraat's kingdom depended upon this general's valour. She could not afford to displease him. On the other hand, it was also not possible to send Sairandhri to Keechak, as she had already laid a clear condition that she will not serve any unknown male. The queen, after much thought, took the way out and said, "Keechak, call on Sairandhri yourself and win her heart."

While Keechak was visiting the queen, Sairandhri had gone there to serve him some wine. Keechak then tried to grab her. Managing to escape, Sairandhri fled to the main courtroom of Viraat. Keechak followed her, and in full view of others, tried to manhandle her. 'Kank' Yudhishthir was quite angry at this sight, but somehow restrained himself.

Later on, Sairandhri went to Ballav in the kitchen and told him of her plight. He assured,

"Do not panic. Keechak shall be taught a lesson. Just ask him to come to the *natakshala* tomorrow night. Leave the rest to me."

Sairandhri met Keechak and told him accordingly. He was mightily pleased with this sudden turn. At the appointed time however in place of Sairandhri, Bheem lay in wait – wrapped in a saree, pretending to be asleep. Keechak was quite drunk even before nightfall. At night, he went there and being under influence and due to the darkness there, mistook the sleeping Bheem for Sairandhri and began to make advances. Bheem grabbed him by his hair, and banging his head on the wall, killed him.

Thus Keechak was slain and Droupadi's honour was saved by Bheem. But the widespread news was that the five invisible Gandharv husbands of Sairandhri had punished Keechak for his mischief against their wife.

‖ End of the *Adnyatvaas* ‖

Keechak's end was a big news which spread like wild fire. Susharma, the king of the nearby country Trigarta, also heard the news. The feud between Viraat and Susharma was an old one; and Susharma was lying low only because he was afraid of Viraat's army chief, Keechak. Now with Keechak gone, he felt that he had an excellent chance to make the score even with Viraat; and approached Duryodhan.

Susharma requested,

" O Kourav supremo! We have an excellent opportunity to attack Viraat and steal his cattle-stock and other wealth. Please assist me in this venture. You may add something to your coffers and I shall get the opportunity to take revenge on Viraat."

Karna too liked this line of thinking of Susharma. Duryodhan readied the Kourav army. Getting news of a possible attack, Viraat also prepared his forces for a possible conflict. Viraat himself, accompanied by Yudhishthir, Bheem, Nakul, Sahadeo went to the battleground. A fierce battle ensued. With the Kouravs helping Susharma, Viraat was finding the going tough and had to withdraw. At one point, it seemed that Viraat himself would become a captive of the enemy.

Yudhishthir was worried at this situation. How would it do that the king finds himself surrounded and on the point of defeat, even when five Pandavs were present on his side? He signalled Bheem to go into offensive. Accordingly, Bheem mounted an attack and made the army of Susharma run away.

But in the meantime, Duryodhan – aided by Bheeshma, Drona, Karna and others had begun driving away the cattle of Viraat from the other side. There was nobody to cover this flank of the Viraat army. Viraat's son Uttar however was busy boasting at home that he would have finished off the Kouravs if only he had a proper charioteer to go with him. Arjun was quite eager to get into a fight against the Kouravs. He did some mental calculation, and realized that the period of remaining *incognito* was over. He said to the boastful prince, "I am willing to become your charioteer. Come, let us see how you fight with the Kouravs!"

Arjun then put the prince in a chariot and drove the chariot straight to the battleground. Before reaching there, he went by the graveyard and collected his weapons from the hollow of the Shami tree. When he saw the expanse of the Kourav army, Prince Uttar found it hard to sustain his bravado: hardly able to speak, he just sat there. Arjun then reassured him, asked him just to hold on to the reins of the chariot, and began his characteristic shower of arrows on the enemy, accompanied by the loud twang of his bow Gandeev. By his mere presence and the sound of his conch and the Gandeev, the Kourav army was frightened and began running helter-skelter.

With Arjun's arrival on the battlefront, the plight of Karna, Dusshaasan and Ashvatthaama was also miserable. Witnessing this unexpected burst of bravery from the other side, *pitamaha* Bheeshma said to Duryodhan, "This brave warrior in woman's clothes must only be Arjun. The one-year period of Pandavs' *adnyatvaas* is over; and, if it is Arjun we are fighting with, it is very difficult to turn the tide against him now." Duryodhan did not like this speech, and he kept on fighting. But ultimately, he had to accept defeat against Arjun's bravery.

After the victorious conclusion of the battle against the Kouravs, Arjun entered the capital to the accompaniment of loud sounds of drums and trumpets. The whole city celebrated the victory like a festival.

King Viraat and Yudhishthir were sitting at the court at that time, playing dice. On hearing the sounds of the victory festival, Yudhishthir said, "Brihannada made this victory possible, my Lord!"

The king did not like this remark going against his son and in a fit of temper, threw a piece of the dice at Yudhishthir. It hit him on the face and he started bleeding. Just then, Sairandhri came there. Since convention has it that the blood of a crowned king should not be spilt on the ground, she quickly held a pot under the flowing blood and prevented its spilling. Uttar then came in along with Arjun. He also told that Brihannada's help made the victory possible, and King Viraat was surprised.

By now the Pandavs were free to reveal their true identity. Seeing the likes of Yudhishthir, Bheem, Arjun, Droupadi before him, King Viraat was ashamed. He said, "Kindly pardon me, if I have done anything to offend you, O brave ones!"

Yudhishthir however said to him, "You need not apologize, King Viraat. On the contrary, we should be grateful to you for the year-long shelter you gave us."

Viraat then sought to perpetuate the relationship he now had with the Pandavs, and offered his daughter in marriage to Arjun. Arjun however refused immediately, saying, Uttara was now like a daughter to him. Yudhishthir suggested a way out, "Arjun is quite right in treating Uttara like a daughter. Make her his daughter-in-law by marrying her with Arjun's son Abhimanyu: it is both proper and benefitting to our relationship."

It was thus decided to get Abhimanyu and Uttara married.

The marriage ceremony brought together all the relations of the Pandavs, barring of course the Kourav cousins. Both uncles, Balram and Shrikrishna, were present. Grandfather Drupad had also come down. They all were happy that the Pandavs had successfully passed through the 12-year *vanvaas* and one-year period of *adnyatvaas*. After the marriage ceremony was duly completed, the well-wishers naturally began discussing what the Pandavs should do henceforth and where they should reside. Yudhishthir said, "You all are senior and wise people. Kindly advise us as to what we should do."

Shrikrishna said, "Pandavs had failed in the game of dice. They have abided by the conditions laid, and have completed twelve years of exile and one year of *incognito* stay. Now it only seems fit and proper that the Kouravs should return to them half the kingdom. After all, this is an internal matter of the Kurus. The Pandavs and the Kouravs are brethren. Let the bygones be bygones and now let the enmity be buried."

Everyone liked this sane counsel by Shrikrishna. But Saatyaki said, "Why be so meek? Half the kingdom belongs to the Pandavs by right. If the Kouravs refuse this right, let there be a war – one clean cut blow and two pieces! It will at least decide this issue once and for all."

But Shrikrishna did not want things to go by war's way yet. To him, war was the last solution, to be used only if all other legitimate ways were over. He convinced all present of this approach and said, "King Drupad is the senior-most amongst us all here. He is respected even by the elder Kourav such as Bheeshmacharya and Kripacharya. Let King Drupad send an emissary of his to the Kourav court and open negotiations with the Kouravs."

This suggestion of Shrikrishna was agreeable to all those present. Drupad too conceded to the plan and agreed to do the needful.

‖ Victory Is Where Krishna Is! ‖

King Drupad had undertaken a difficult task. Accordingly, he sent his court-priest to Hastinapur to the Kourav court for negotiations. If the peace talks succeed, nothing like it. But if they fail, it means war. Thus one should know who all are on our side, and which kings would be of help. So to gauge this, messengers were sent beforehand to various countries.

Assistance from Shrikrishna was of utmost importance. Hence Arjun decided to go to Dwaraka and make a formal request to Krishna for help.

As the Pandavs were preparing for a possible war, Duryodhan too was not keeping quiet. He too was shrewd and reached Dwaraka. Shrikrishna was in a predicament, finding that Arjun and Duryodhan both had reached him simultaneously for the same purpose. But he very cleverly extricated himself from the tricky situation. As a matter of fact, from the heart of his heart, Krishna wanted to be on the side of the Pandavs. For theirs was the side of truth, equity and justice. Yet he wanted to test both Duryodhan and Arjun. He told them both, whosoever comes before my eyes first after I rise from my siesta in the third *prahar**, I shall go to his side.

As Shrikrishna lay on the bed for the siesta, Duryodhan came there. He chose to sit towards the headside of the bed, as it was more prestigious – more suitable to his king-like status. He also felt that he would be the first one before Shrikrishna as he opened his eyes. Arjun on the other hand was a simple person; moreover, he was a disciple of Shrikrishna. He felt that his place is at the feet of the Lord. He sat humbly by Shrikrishna's feet.

Shrikrishna arose after a while and as he opened his eyes, his gaze fell first on Arjun. "When did you come, Arjun?" he asked getting up. Then he saw Duryodhan sitting at the other side of the bed. But the first pick of choice in the matter of Shrikrishna's help was already decided. But did Duryodhan really want to have Shrikrishna in person? He wanted the massive Yadav army.

Duryodhan said, "I did not expect you to come to my side anyway. But I want your army."

Shrikrishna heard it, and laughed to himself. He said, "What is your desire, Arjun?"

Arjun promptly replied, "I want nothing but you, Krishna!"

After a while Duryodhan left, and Shrikrishna asked Arjun,

"You are out to fight a war, Arjun. Then how is it that you preferred me, alone, over and above my numerous army?"

Arjun whereupon replied, "I know for certain, O Mukund, that victory is where Shrikrishna is!"

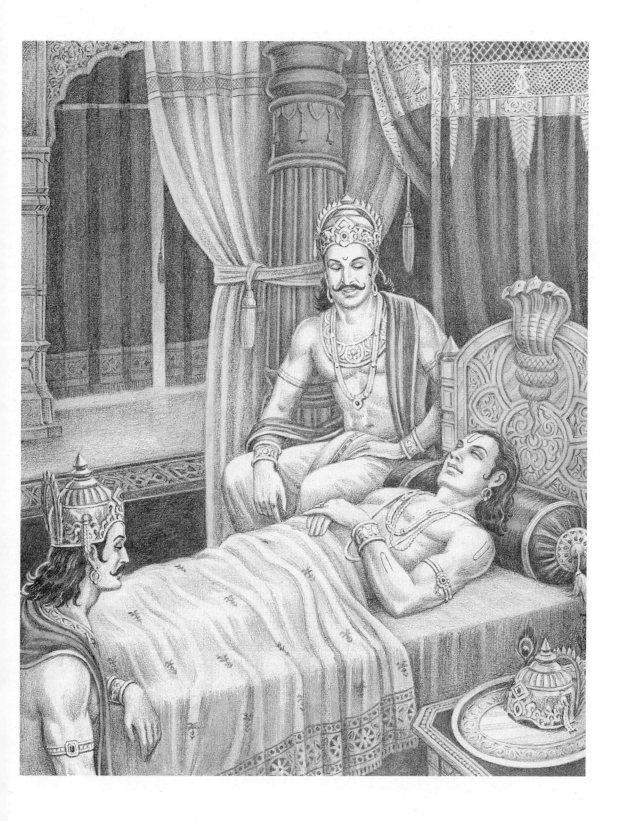

|| The Diplomacy of Krishna ||

The court priest, the Guruji, sent by King Drupad reached Hastinapur. He duly put forth the say of the Pandavs before Bheeshma, Dhritarashtra, Drona, Kripa, Vidur and others. He requested, "Let the Pandavs have their half of the kingdom and let us put an end to the conflict among the brethren." All seemed to be in favour of the proposal and showed their consent.

But Duryodhan did not approve of it one bit. Karna also sided with him and did his best to fan the hatred against Pandavs in Duryodhan's mind. Bheeshma, Dhritarashtra and Drona tried their best to reason with Duryodhan, but he adamantly kept his own counsel. "Once we have defeated the Pandavs, their kingdom is ours. Let them come and win it back from us through war; then we will see," said Duryodhan.

The court priest returned empty-handed.

Even though Duryodhan was so adamant and hard in his stand, Shrikrishna wanted to make one final effort to win his mind and avert the war. For war, after all, hurts both sides – the destruction is on both sides.

Thus Shrikrishna himself came to Hastinapur to try his diplomacy with the Kouravs. Duryodhan wanted to treat him lavishly, but Shrikrishna chose to stay with Vidur.

The Pandavs had told Shrikrishna before he set out for Hastinapur. "Please do not suffer insults for our sake". But Shrikrishna maintained that he did not care about personal glory or insult when it came to the larger welfare of many.

When the Kouravs were at court, Shrikrishna entered their meeting and tried to convince them how the Pandavs represented truth and justice. All elders, sages and kings present in the meeting hall praised Shrikrishna's speech and expressed their consent to what he was saying. Shrikrishna also warned what internal struggle was likely to lead to. This prediction was seconded by sages such as Kanva and Narad.

Then Dhritarashtra maintained, "I agree to all that is being said. But you better convince Duryodhan about it." Shrikrishna and other elders tried again to persuade Duryodhan. They said that the Pandavs could do with only five villages to avoid war.

But Duryodhan had gone blind and senseless with a burning hatred for the Pandavs, and could not be convinced. He flared up and said, "Pandavs are only five in number, we are a hundred. Before seeking a thing one should see what his ability is. We are not willing to part even a little speck of earth that can remain on a needlepoint, leave alone five villages!"

Upon these words, without losing calm Shrikrishna said, "It seems that you are bound to witness the decimation of the entire Kuru family tree. Wisdom lies in giving to the Pandavs what is rightfully their due. Or else, be prepared for war; and remember, in the war, your destruction is certain. For ultimately, it is always truth that prevails, and the Pandav claim is a true one."

After being rebuked thus by Shrikrishna, Duryodhan, Dusshaasan, Karna, Shakuni left the court, shouting angrily and sticking to their claims.

Shrikrishna then suggested at the court that it would be advisable to arrest Duryodhan, Dusshaasan to avoid the complete destruction of Kurus.

But, on the other side, the angry ones that had walked out were plotting to arrest and put Shrikrishna in prison. Saatyaki informed Shrikrishna, as well as Dhritarashtra and Vidur, about the conspiracy. Dhritarashtra immediately recalled Duryodhan to the court. Here Shrikrishna manifested before the court the many divine powers that he possessed (so that none of them should entertain any false hopes of imprisoning him) and went back to Viraat's capital where the Pandavs were staying.

‖ Kunti Meets Karna ‖

While leaving Hastinapur, Shrikrishna had called Karna aside and had told him, "Karna, you too are my cousin."

An astonished Karna asked, "How come?"

Shrikrishna then told Karna the story of his birth. "You are the firstborn of Kunti. You were born of the great mantra that she had received from the sage. Thus Kunti is your mother, and you are the eldest of the Pandavs," he informed.

"Only because you say it, I might believe it, Krishna," replied Karna. "But even if it is true, how can I regard Kunti as my mother? For fear of people's extreme criticism, she threw me off in water as soon as I was born. It was only the *soota* Adhirath and his wife Radha who raised and nurtured me. Thus for me, Adhirath and Radha are father and mother. Duryodhan too treated me as an equal, and made friends with me, honoured me by making me a king. What status I have today is due to him. It would be a sacrilege if I quit him now. It would be like betraying and destroying a friend."

Some time later, one day while Karna had just finished his bath and was offering the *arghya* to the Sun, Kunti arrived there. She was quite upset since she had heard that the mediation by Shrikrishna had failed and war was unavoidable. She had premonitions of the terrible destruction that was to take place in the ensuing war. She wished with all her heart that the war should be averted, destruction avoided. But who would have listened to her? She was making a last effort to convince at least Karna, the *maharathi** by telling him the truth, and winning him over to the side of the Pandavs.

"Karna, my son!" She called out with great affection.

"Who is it?" asked Karna.

"Kunti, your mother, " said Kunti.

"Yes, I know. But though you have given me birth, it is now Radha who is my mother in the true sense."

"You should forget this part of your life," Kunti said.

"How can I? These are things that just cannot be forgotten," Karna replied.

"So will you fight against your real blood-brothers?"

"Now my brothers are Duryodhan, Dusshaasan... all the Kouravs. They were the ones who gave me love and affection that is due from brothers. Now I belong to them. I cannot desert them. Thus your efforts to convince me are in vain, *mataji*."

"If the Pandavs win, as the eldest, you shall be entitled to the kingdom. They shall gladly concede to your claim."

"I do not want such a kingdom. Yudhishthir may well enjoy it!"

With the firmness of Karna, Kunti was astonished. She kept quiet for a while. Then she said,

"Let us leave this argument at that. But just as you are famous for your bravery, you are also known for generosity. They say your generosity is boundless."

"What is it that you desire, mother?"

"I want the Pandavs to survive. Do not kill any of them."

With this demand, Karna also was silent. He was touched by the mother's love for her sons. He said, "There will be no killing as far as Yudhishthir, Bheem, Nakul and Sahadeo. But I must fight with Arjun. That is a vow I have taken long back. So any whichever way our battle goes, you shall have five sons. There is no point in your insisting anything otherwise."

Kunti had nothing to say now. She returned disheartened.

|| Ready for War ||

The war was a certainty now. Immediately on his return, Shrikrishna told the Pandavs that they had no other way but to fight for truth and justice.

At the word from Shrikrishna, the Pandavs began assembling their forces. The kings who were in their camp came with their armies. Drishtadyumna, son of Drupad, was made the chief of the Pandav army as suggested by Shrikrishna.

The Kouravs too were preparing in right earnest. Their supporter-kings came with their armies. The Kouravs requested *pitamaha* Bheeshma to lead their army. Upon this request Bheeshma said, "Since I am one of your courtiers, and as I am governed by the rules of statecraft, I concede to your request. Otherwise, to me, both the Pandavs and Kouravs, are equal and the same. Yet I shall fight as asked, on two conditions."

"Which ones?"

"I shall kill only ten thousand warriors of the enemy per day," said Bheeshma.

"And your other condition?"

"On the battleground, it shall be either Karna or myself. I cannot fight where Karna is also there in the side."

Karna was very angry at this condition and said, "It is okay. I shall fight only after the fall of Bheeshma."

After both armies were ready, certain rules of the war were laid down. Both the armies had four sections – infantry, cavalry, elephant-riders and those driving chariots. The rules laid down that only equals shall fight; only a soldier from infantry could fight against each other and so on; none should be killed by catching unawares, someone who has surrendered should not be killed. Both sides agreed to abide by them.

Both the armies stood on the battleground Kurukshetra facing each other. The Pandav army was made up of seven *akshouhinis* and the Kouravs, eleven *akshouhinis*.

Shrikrishna himself drove the chariot of Arjun. He took the chariot right in the centre of the battlefield, between both the armies. At a glance on the enemy army, Arjun could see Bheeshma, Drona, Kripa and relations; elderly and respectable persons. Seeing them ahead as enemies in the battleground, Arjun felt, 'Now I shall be forced to use my weapons against them; destruction shall certainly ensue and if we win, it shall have to be through the blood of venerable persons. No, no! It is not the right thing to do – it is outright evil!'

At this thought, Arjun lost all his drive to fight. He became as if a clod of earth. He said to Shrikrishna, "Lord, I cannot fight this war. What use is the kingdom and glory that comes by killing the near and dear ones? No, Krishna, I shall not fight, I shall not perform this evil action."

Seeing the misery of Arjun, Shrikrishna reassured, "Wherefrom has this cowardice engulfed you on the battleground, O Arjun? It is not at all appropriate for a valiant person like you. You must remember, Parth, that this war is not being fought for anyone's personal gain: it is a clash of two principles.

"When a war is fought for some principle, you must pay attention to what your duty is. Your feeling that you shall end all these great persons is not true; it is merely substanceless shadow. Remember, whosoever has greater principles, his duty is equally great. Whether it is Bheeshma, Dronacharya or any one else, remember even before you kill them, they are already dead by choosing the side of falsehood; and have lost their principles. The establishment of truth has to be preceded by destruction of those with no principles or those who have taken to wrong principles.

"Arjun, do not labour under any false delusions and do not entertain any imaginary worries. While performing one's duty, one must remain free from anger, hatred, attachment or lust – the six disorders of oneself and do one's duty come what may. Action taken should not be polluted with the hankering for the fruit of the act, it should be a clean action. Therefore Arjun, arise, take up your bow; blow your mighty conch to terrify the enemy!"

With these words and such advice from Shrikrishna, Arjun became free from the confusion he was enmeshed and his brave arms began to aspire for the real action.

The advice leading to duty and genuine religion, given by Shrikrishna to Arjun, is famous as 'Shrimad Bhagwad-Geeta'.

|| On the Battlefield ||

Before the actual battle began, Yudhishthir got down from his chariot and started walking towards the enemy army. It was indeed a great surprise to all. The Kouravs, seeing him come, felt that he was about to surrender, even before the battle began. But this was Yudhishthir at his righteous best. He was going to the enemy army to bow low before the seniors and seek their blessings before the battle. He first went to the chariot of *pitamaha* Bheeshma and saluted him. Bheeshma was quite pleased with this behaviour and blessed him. Likewise, Dharmaraj received blessings from Dronacharya too.

All were now ready for the battle. At the peak of the battle fever, Bheem was shouting aloud. With his cries, the whole battleground was booming with echoes. Even elephants and horses of the Kourav army were frightened and started trembling. This upset the Kouravs such as Dusshaasan very much and they began showering Bheem with missiles. Simultaneously, there arose the sound of clarions, conchs and battle-drums in the ground. Arrows were set upon bows and sent shooting across the ground. Chariots banged upon chariots, and weapons clanged together.

On the very first day, Uttar, the son of Viraat, came down in the fight against Shalya. Seeing his brother die, Shweta attacked Shalya and killed him with a mighty arrow. The brave lad Shweta had also brought down the flagstaff off Bheeshma's chariot. Finally, Bheeshma had to deploy an arrow on him with the dreaded *Brahma-astra* and Shweta lay dead.

On the second day of the battle, Shrikrishna took Arjun's chariot right up to that of *pitamaha* Bheeshma. The two warriors had a day-long terrible fight.

In the meantime, Bheem made a mincemeat of the brave Kalinga warriors with his mace.

The third day saw an unexpected encounter between Bheem and Duryodhan. Receiving spirited blows from Bheem, Duryodhan fell unconscious. Seeing this the Kourav army was demoralized and they began to disperse. On gaining consciousness, Duryodhan saw this debacle and spoke stinging words of bitter criticism to Bheeshma. He increased the intensity of his arrows so much that many Pandav warriors died. Even Arjun proved ineffective before this renewed offensive tactic of Bheeshma.

One day Shrikrishna took out his *Sudarshan-chakra* and charged it towards Bheeshma. Arjun saw this sight upon regaining consciousness and ran to stop Shrikrishna from breaking vow of non-fighting. He then began his fight against Bheeshma with an added intensity and resolution. Until the eighth day, the battle was nothing else but a direct fight between Arjun and Bheeshma.

On the ninth day, Shikhandi came into the battle (Shikhandi was Princess Amba in the former birth and knowing this, Bheeshma did not raise his weapon against Shikhandi treating him as a woman.) Arjun continued to shower arrows from behind Shikhandi and finally Bheeshma became unconscious with a number of arrows in his body. So many were the arrows in his body, that even though he collapsed, his body did not touch the ground! He lay as if on the bed of arrows. Bheeshma had been given the boon to choose the time of his death. He chose to die till the auspicious *uttaraayan** began, and rested on the same arrow-bed. Arjun then sent down an arrow in such a manner that the spring of water gushing out of the ground directly sent a trickle of water to the dying warrior's mouth. His head was propped up on another of Arjun's arrows.

|| Chakravyooha and Killing Jayadrath ||

On Bheeshma's fall, Dronacharya became the commander of the Kourav army. He vowed that he shall capture Yudhishthir alive. Shrikrishna then made Bheem the commander of the Pandav army. A fierce battle ensued where Drona had arranged the Kourav army in such a circular style *(chakravyooha)* that it would engulf the target in it.

Breaking through such a fielding of warriors required a special type of knowledge, which only Arjun and Shrikrishna were well-versed in. But Drona arranged the battle in such a way that both of them would be engaged in a battle with a chosen band of fourteen thousand warriors on the other side of the battlefield.

Arjun's brave son, Abhimanyu, had half-acquired the knowledge regarding *chakravyooha*. His understanding of the *vyooha* stopped at entering the heart of the circular design, but he did not know how to get out of it. Regardless, the brave lad entered the *chakravyooha,* assured by his uncle Bheem and others that they will follow him and help him through. But they could not keep behind him. Thus Abhimanyu remained all alone in the heart of the *vyooha,* fighting a number of Kourav warriors.

As per instructions of Duryodhan, seven *maharathi*s – Drona, Kripa, Shakuni, Ashvatthaama, Karna, Dusshaasan plus Duryodhan himself came together and killed the lonely lad. It was the thirteenth day of the battle. To add insult to injury, Jayadrath kicked Abhimanyu in the head as he lay dying. On return, Arjun learnt all this and was extremely angry. He vowed on the spot that he shall behead Jayadrath by the next day, or shall die himself by entering a bed of fire!

When the Kouravs learnt of Arjun's vow, they made every arrangement to protect Jayadrath throughout the day. Arjun, aided by Shrikrishna, kept hunting the battleground for Jayadrath all day, but he was nowhere to be seen. Bheem too set out looking for Jayadrath. When he was thwarted by the Kouravs in this, he killed many Kourav warriors.

It was getting dark. The Kouravs now felt that Arjun would take his own life as per his vow. All preparations were made and the fire was lit. To witness this end of Arjun, the Kouravs gathered in large numbers. Jayadrath, too, was there. Seeing Jayadrath among those present, Shrikrishna took away the temporary cover with which he had covered the Sun. Immediately there was light, and Shrikrishna said, "See the Sun is here, and so is Jayadrath."

Within the blink of an eye, Arjun's arrow shot out and Jayadrath was killed. Arjun's vow was fulfilled.

|| Killing of Ghatotkach ||

When his brother-in-law Jayadrath met such an end, Duryodhan was very angry. On that day, he continued the war even after nightfall, contrary to the rules. His instructions to his warriors were to attack the Pandav army even at night and take revenge. Both armies continued their assaults on each other in the dark of night. Ashvatthaama was particularly successful that night, and Duryodhan was goading him on for further destruction.

On the Pandav side, Shrikrishna encouraged the son of Bheem – Ghatotkach – to display his bravery. Ghatotkach's fighting was full of miracles. The more the night progressed, the more effective his tricks were. One moment he would soar high up in the air, the next moment he would assume the form of a hefty elephant and would crash down on to the hapless Kourav army. Another moment he was full of thunder and lightning, frightening the enemy; the next moment he would blind them with a mighty flash. He would move from place to place on the battlefield with the speed of lightning; and it was difficult for the enemy to even aim a weapon at him.

His miracles were confusing the enemy all the time. Even Karna and Duryodhan were not spared from this effect of Ghatotkach's miracles. Innumerable members of the Kourav army were killed; and Duryodhan was afraid that the entire Kourav army would get wiped out through the night. Finally he instructed Karna, "Time has come to use the *Vaasavi-shakti**, the special weapon given to you by Lord Sun himself. Finish this demon."

Karna said, "But I have reserved it for the ultimate battle with Arjun."

Duryodhan was desperate. He said, "We'll see what to do about Arjun, if and when we survive this night of terror."

Karna chanted and called up the *Vaasavi-shakti* and deployed it onto Ghatotkach.

When Ghatotkach saw the fierce *shakti* coming at him, he knew he was no match for such a weapon and was prepared to die. But even while doing so, he assumed a mammoth form; and crashed like a mountain on the Kourav army. Even in death, he killed several scores of people.

The death of Ghatotkach brought gloom over the Pandav camp. But Shrikrishna heaved a sigh of relief. Indeed, he seemed to be happy. When the Pandavs asked him about it, he said, "Now Arjun is out of danger. The divine *shakti*, which was expended in killing Ghatotkach tonight, was to have been used by Karna in his fight against Arjun. Now Karna is left without any special weapons."

Thus even the worst thing gives rise to some good. On this note, the death of Ghatotkach ended that day's battle.

|| End of Drona ||

Duryodhan, going to the extreme, asked Dronacharya to kill the Pandavs by using the ultimate weapon, *Brahma-astra*. Dronacharya therefore was fighting with utmost intensity. Following the end of Ghatotkach, he took two major prizes: he killed Drupad and Viraat. This naturally made the Pandavs furious. Drishtadyumna particularly, was afire with the idea of revenge. He announced, "I shall kill Drona somehow or the other today; or else I shall go to Hell!"

There was a terrible fight. Drishtadyumna literally showered Drona with arrows, but they were of no use.

Shrikrishna told them, "As long as Dronacharya is holding any weapon in his hand, it is impossible to defeat him. And there is just one way to make him weaponless. That is, to make him know that Ashvatthaama, his son, is no more."

Bheem liked this idea of Shrikrishna. Shouting aloud, he went and killed an elephant, also by the name Ashvatthaama, belonging to the King of Malav from their own camp. Then approaching Dronacharya, he told him,

"Bad news, Acharya! Ashvatthaama is killed!"

Hearing this news, Drona's mind was filled with grief for his son to the brim. He was heartbroken. But to make sure if the news was true or false, he went near the chariot of Yudhishthir. True to his other name, Dharmaraj, Yudhishthir was a man of principles, always speaking nothing but the truth, Drona believed. He asked Yudhishthir,

"Dharma, is it true that Ashvatthaama is killed?"

Yudhishthir replied, "Yes, Acharya. It is true that Ashvatthaama is killed, but..."

He uttered the other part of the sentence in a low voice. "It is not known whether it is the man or an elephant."

In the din of the battle, Drona hardly had the presence of mind left to listen to this vital rider added at the end. He just laid down his arms and sat in his chariot, deep in grief.

Taking this opportunity, Drishtadyumna mounted the chariot of Drona. Holding the flowing silvery hair of Drona in one hand, with the other hand he cut off Drona's head.

It was indeed a terrible sight. Ashvatthaama was so furious that he took out the *Narayan-astra* and fired it on the Pandavs. Shrikrishna saw it coming and knew what to do. He asked each and every fighting man to drop his weapon immediately and stand with folded hands. It was the speciality of this *astra* that it never killed anyone who was not wielding a weapon and was in the saluting position. The extremely powerful weapon also proved ineffective.

But Ashvatthaama made a terrible vow, there and then, to end the Pandav family.

|| The Karna Era ||

Following the slaying of Dronacharya, Duryodhan was very sad. He had lost his morale. Seeing him sit and worry like this, Ashvatthaama said to him, "When you have a fine warrior like Karna on your side, what makes you so desperate? It is time you entrusted the baton of the Kourav army commander to Karna."

Duryodhan approved of this suggestion. Promptly approaching Karna, he said to him, "Karna, now the fortune of the Kouravs rests entirely upon you. After the fall of Bheeshma and Drona, you should now accept the command of the Kourav army. After all, both of them were drawn to the Pandavs inwardly. Now you could apply all the skill at your command and finish off the Pandavs."

Upon this, Karna said, "As per your suggestion, I shall take command of the Kourav army."

Duryodhan was quite pleased and exclaimed, "Then the victory of Kouravs is ensured!"

"But it is not so easy," Karna interrupted, "I might be a better warrior than any Pandav due to my skill with weapons. But I have a great lacuna in that I do not have someone like Shrikrishna driving my chariot."

"What can we do in this matter, Karna?"

"We have only one person as skilful as Shrikrishna in driving the chariot," said Karna.

"Who is that?" Duryodhan asked.

"Shalya!"

Hearing Karna's choice, Duryodhan immediately approached Shalya and pleaded with him, "It is a crisis now. So brave warrior, kindly agree to do this one thing for me."

"Tell me, what can I do for you?" Shalya asked.

"Be Karna's charioteer," Duryodhan replied.

Shalya was mad with anger at this suggestion. He took this as a personal insult, and said with contempt,

"Myself, a crowned king; and I should drive the chariot of that *sootaputra*? Never, never!"

But Duryodhan pleaded and cajoled him so much that Shalya consented but only after laying down a condition. He said,

"Karna shall have to listen to whatever I say, without a single complaint or protest. Is that understood?"

Duryodhan agreed to this condition in order to get Shalya to do the needful.

Thus Karna, the commander of the Kourav army, being taken around in the chariot of Shalya, began shouting slogans, "Where is Arjun? Show me that warrior and I... "

Shalya said to him curtly, "Karna, why do you boast for nothing? All your bravado is in vain. Do you think people have forgotten your running away from many battlegrounds to avoid Arjun's arrows?"

Thus, Shalya would run Karna down and insult him at the crucial moment. He even went to the extent of comparing Karna with a crow fattened on the leftovers. Before real arrows, Karna was seriously hurt within by the verbal arrows shot by Shalya.

Finally, the chariot bearing Karna was piloted by Shalya to the middle of the battleground between the Kourav and Pandav armies. Due to the insults, Karna was already boiling with rage. Like the storm in the ocean, he attacked Yudhishthir's chariot the moment his eyes fell on him. He tore apart Yudhishthir's flag, broke the string of his bow, and also the chariot, and injured the charioteer immensely.

Yudhishthir made all the earnest efforts to keep up with Karna's fury, but finally he had to give up. Turning his back on the battle, he began taking his chariot back to the pavilion. Karna then laughed aloud with derision and said, "Go away, Yudhishthir! Go while I have taken pity on you and am letting you live!"

This insulting treatment was a sharp stinging blow to Yudhishthir's mind.

By then, Arjun had finished fighting with the select Samshaptak warriors. On his return, he observed from a long distance and found that Yudhishthir's flag did not flutter amidst the Pandav army. He was worried. Entrusting the battleground to Bheem for a while, he decided to go to the pavilion. Shrikrishna and Arjun came to the pavilion.

Dharmaraj Yudhishthir, who was recovering in the pavilion, narrated all that had happened, to Arjun. Arjun set out with Yudhishthir's blessings with a vow to kill Karna in the battle.

|| Killing of Dusshaasan ||

By the time Arjun returned to the battleground, Bheem and Dusshaasan had advanced deep in their duel.

It was Bheem's vow to administer the capital punishment to Dusshaasan for his misdeeds and he was eager to fulfill it. On the other hand, Dusshaasan also had an intense hatred for Bheem. Both the mighty warriors were doing their best to outdo each other.

They kept on trying all designs-counterdesigns against each other, as also, using all types of missiles against the foe. Many a time, Dusshaasan lost consciousness by the hot arrows of Bheem. Bheem too, had become livid with rage when Dusshaasan's arrows hit home.

In such a furious battle, one of the arrows from Dusshaasan hit Bheem to the core. Bheem then jumped down from his chariot in a fit of rage with his mace in hand. Moving the mace around, high in the air, several times, with its single blow he brought Dusshaasan down to the ground.

Then, as the foe lay facing the skies, Bheem planted his pillar-like leg hard on Dusshaasan's chest. Then, unsheathing his sword, he shouted,

"You devil! Are not you the one who ran us down in the Kourav court? Moreover, are not these the evil hands that dragged poor Droupadi by her hair? You were the devil who dared to pull her clothes too! Now pay for all those evil deeds. Enjoy your deserts!"

With these words, Bheem uprooted the right hand of the fallen Dusshaasan with one mighty jerk, and threw it off. Then he hit him hard on his chest, breaking it open. Even as the blood spurting from Dusshaasan's heart was warm, Bheem scooped up handfuls and drank it! He had fulfilled his vow.

Afterwards, Bheem cut off Dusshaasan's head and hurled it towards the Kourav army.

Then, shouting slogans and thumping arms, Bheem proceeded towards the battleground to wreak havoc into the enemy.

Having killed Dusshaasan, the next item on Bheem's list was the Kourav supremo Duryodhan. He was waiting for this fight and blood raced through his mighty arms as he looked forward to the ultimate battle.

‖ End of Karna ‖

On the other battlefront, a duel was going on between Karna's son, Vrishsen, and Nakul. Feelings were running high since Abhimanyu was killed cruelly, and both warriors were making utmost efforts to win the battle.

Vrishsen was a fine archer; and Nakul started lagging behind before the onslaught of his arrows. Just then, Arjun came there. When he saw the scene where Karna's son was on the offensive, targeting Karna, Arjun said,

"You seven senior Kourav *maharathi*s together killed my son Abhimanyu by catching him alone in the *chakravyooha*, Karna! Now see how I alone kill your son Vrishsen."

With these words, Arjun's mighty arrow flew off, going straight through the delicate neck of Vrishsen.

Karna was angry at this terrible spectacle. Just then Shalya said, "Karna! Your enemy Arjun is right before you. So let us see how you show him your valour. Go ahead!"

Karna was raring to go and finish Arjun off; on the other hand, Arjun also wanted to put an end to their tussle for supremacy once and for all. Krishna, encouraging Arjun in this duel, told him, "Buck up, Arjun. Do your best!"

It was a fierce battle between two reputed warriors, Arjun and Karna. As they confronted each other, both the Kourav and Pandav armies as if forgetting to fight just stood looking on. Both were brave, and mighty archers. Both had excellent command on the art of missiles and weaponry.

With arrows clashing from each side, a fierce battle ensued. When Arjun deployed the *Agneya-astra*, Karna quenched its fire by sending off the rain missile *Parjanya-astra*. Arjun's *Vajra-astra* was rendered ineffective by Karna's *Bhargav-astra*.

As the battle thus progressed, a strange thing took place.

The wheel of Karna's chariot was gobbled up by the earth. As the wheel was stuck in the mud, the chariot would not move.

Seeing this, Karna jumped down from the chariot and started desperate efforts to lift up the wheel. Arjun had in the meantime, readied his bow once again. Karna requested,

"Wait, Arjun! Wait till I lift up the wheel of my chariot from this mire. My hands are otherwise occupied. I am holding no weapon, and so am unarmed. It is not proper to attack someone who is unarmed."

Listening to this request by Karna, Shrikrishna laughed and said, "A fine time you have chosen to preach ethics, Karna! You did not think whether it is proper, trying to disrobe Droupadi in full view of the whole court; or when you tried to poison the Pandavs; or when you tried to burn them as they slept in the Lakshagrih. Nor was religion any bar when you cheated a saintly soul like Yudhishthir in the game of dice. Where was your sense of right and wrong then, Karna?"

Karna was too confused to answer. And what could he possibly answer? He felt, that his end had come near. Desperately, he tried to remember the powerful *astras* which he had obtained from Parashuram. But he could not remember any. His intellect lost all lustre, and his body was becoming weak.

Shrikrishna said, "Arjun! Shoot your arrow."

Arjun's Gandeev bow was ready. He sent out a powerful arrow. The arrow flew and cut off Karna's head high in the air within a moment!

With Karna's end, Shalya returned to the pavilion with the empty chariot. Duryodhan was shocked to hear this news. He fainted with the impact of the tragic event.

Shalya's Command Comes to an End

Their king lay unconscious, and the commander of the army was killed. The Kourav army was rudderless, trembling in fear. Moreover, Bheem had gone on a spree of killing every other Kourav warrior.

Totally lacking in morale, the Kourav army started running here and there. There was a total confusion. In the meantime, Duryodhan regained consciousness.

Seeing the debacle in the army, he said,

"Do not run. And where can you run away, after all? You are not going to be spared, even if you run. The Pandavs shall now hunt for you to the land's end and kill you anyway. Rather than dying like cowards, fight bravely in the battleground and attain better status after death!"

"We admit, our end is near, King Duryodhan. We also agree that we should die fighting, if death is inevitable. But under whose guidance shall we fight?" asked the Kourav warriors.

Duryodhan thereupon replied,

"Shalya, crowned King of the Madra country, is now the commander of the Kourav army. Regroup yourselves under his banner and fight with the Pandavs till the end."

Even after this much destruction, Duryodhan's craving to shed blood for his ambition's sake was not yet fulfilled.

As per Duryodhan's request, Shalya took over the reins of what little Kourav army remained. He faced the Pandav army the next day with full preparation.

Shrikrishna then said to Yudhishthir, "This is your catch today, Yudhishthir."

Yudhishthir replied, "But Krishna, Shalya happens to be our maternal uncle."

"This is the battleground, Yudhishthir, and you are here to fight the enemy," said Shrikrishna, "Here whom you confront is your enemy and those that are fighting by your side are your friends. It is the only relationship that the battlefield recognizes; and wiping off the opponent is the only duty it prescribes. Forget everything else, and do your duty."

"Very well, Mukund!" agreed Yudhishthir and took up his magnificent bow.

There was a fierce fight between Shalya and Yudhishthir. Both did their valiant best to excel each other. Finally, Yudhishthir deployed a mighty *shakti,* and with it Shalya's head flew high in the air and his lifeless body collapsed to the ground.

Shalya was used to riding a mighty elephant who was always in heat. Drishtadyumna floored the elephant with a blow of his mace and cut off the head of Shalva.

Sahadeo obstructed the path of Shakuni who was about to run away. Shakuni was the root-cause of all this destruction of both the Kourav and Pandav armies. He was the one who had, always and consistently, fuelled and fanned Duryodhan's hatred against the Pandavs.

With a single powerful arrow, Sahadeo beheaded Shakuni.

Death of Shalya, Shalva and Shakuni-*mama* was the final straw for the Kourav army. Deserting the battlefield was rampant in the ranks. The Pandav army was catching whosoever they could; and killing them.

|| Duryodhan's Last Battle ||

With all his generals and strong army killed in the great war, Duryodhan was very depressed. He felt miserable. Dark despair clouded his reason; and mace in hand, the once-mighty Kourav ruler ran towards a lake to take refuge there.

There was a sprawling large lake in the east, and in it an island. Duryodhan hid himself there. Kripacharya, Kritavarma and Ashvatthaama knew of the island; and after a long search came to meet him. They said to him,

"If you run away from the battle, what do we do?"

"Only you three have survived, is it not ?" asked Duryodhan.

"Yes. But even just the three of us can offer stiff resistance to the Pandavs. For that, you must remain with us, O King."

"I have had just too much for today. Let me rest, and let us see what to do tomorrow," Duryodhan said.

This conversation was heard by the *vyadhs**, who supplied meat to Bheem every day. They promptly informed him. Hearing it, Bheem as well as all the other Pandavs were glad, as they all were looking for Duryodhan. When they learnt of his hideout, they all came to the lake.

Yudhishthir came forth and said,

"Duryodhan, having caused all this destruction, you run from the battlefield like a coward and hide here. It does not befit you. Come out and face the battle like a man!"

"I am quite tired. I need to rest. I shall fight with all of you tomorrow," said Duryodhan from within his hideout.

"A true warrior gets rest only after the battle is over. Many brave warriors, even elders sacrificed their lives for you; and you talk of rest? Come out and fight, the war has to end now," said Yudhishthir.

Due to Yudhishthir's sermon and the accompanying laughter of the other Pandavs, Duryodhan was stung to the quick. He came out, as a king cobra coming out of his hole.

As soon as Duryodhan came out, a duel ensued between Bheem and Duryodhan. Both were expert mace-fighters, equally strong and adamant, fighting to finish – it was a terrible sight. Sometimes, Duryodhan would faint, unable to sustain a mighty blow from Bheem's mace; on the other hand, Bheem would lose consciousness by a skilful blow from Duryodhan. But as soon as they would come to consciousness, they would re-engage in the fight. The bouts went on for a quite a while, and then Shrikrishna reminded Bheem of his vow through Arjun: Arjun simply touched his own thighs. Reminded of the vow, Bheem administered a massive blow of his mace on Duryodhan's thighs. It simply made mincemeat of his thighs and he collapsed on the ground in acute pain.

As soon as Duryodhan fell, the Pandavs rejoiced heartily. Bheem went forth in rage and kicked him in the head. He said to Duryodhan, "You scoundrel! You were showing Droupadi your thigh in full view of the court, were you not? Now pay for it!"

Thus feeling victorious, Pandavs returned to the pavilion. Reaching there, Shrikrishna asked Arjun to get down from the chariot first. Arjun got down with his bow, and Krishna too took the horses aside, and the chariot burst into flames all of a sudden!

All were surprised to see this sight. Shrikrishna explained,

"As the war went on, so many missiles were thrown at Arjun on this chariot. They were all taken on first by the chariot; and due to my presence, no danger was felt. Now that the war is over, the job of this chariot is also over."

There on the other side, Ashvatthaama was taking a vow before the dying Duryodhan that he will not rest without destroying all the Pandavs that day. Duryodhan thereupon made him the Kourav army commander.

‖ *Revenge! Revenge!* ‖

The camp of the Pandavs was full of festive atmosphere of victory. Till midnight and past, the tales of war were being told and retold. The whole camp went to sleep in the same euphoric state.

Ashvatthaama, on the other hand, lay on his forest bed, thinking all the time of the revenge he wished to take. How should he go about it? How best to annihilate the Pandavs?

In such a state of mind, Ashvatthaama found a remarkable scene being enacted on the nearby tree. Young crows lay fast asleep in the branches, and stealthily coming there, an owl was killing the young ones of the crows one by one, and eating them up.

Gruesome as the scene was, Ashvatthaama was so glad to see it – he had found a cruel but effective way for his revenge. He then awakened Kripa and Kritavarma who were sleeping nearby. He told them how he took a hint from the ways of the owl just seen, and thus finish the Pandavs.

Both Kripacharya and Kritavarma did not like this suggestion of Ashvatthaama. But since he was mad with the idea of revenge, and as he was their leader, as an appointed commander, they followed his orders and proceeded to the Pandav camp.

Coming to the gate of the camp, Ashvatthaama encountered a terrible figure. He tried to kill it, but the weird figure seemed to be immune to all attacks. Ashvatthaama then, invoking Lord Shankar, offered to sacrifice himself in fire, there and then. Shankar then manifested himself there, and gave his blessings and a mighty sword to Ashvatthaama. With it, he went inside the Pandav camp. There he found many Pandav warriors and Drishtadyumna fast asleep. Ashvatthaama first leapt upon the sleeping Drishtadyumna and killed him on the spot. Along with the other Pandav warriors, the five sons of Droupadi, one from each Pandav, were also killed by him as they lay in sleep.

After it, brimming with joy, Ashvatthaama accompanied by Kripa and Krita came to Duryodhan. They told him of the carnage they had perpetrated. Duryodhan was, as if holding on to life, just to hear this news. He died in an unholy bliss, hearing of the complete destruction of the Pandav family tree.

Droupadi's grief knew no bounds when she heard of the killing of her five sons. The Pandavs too were shocked at losing all five sons at once. Droupadi's head was whirring with rage by this ghastly killing spree by Ashvatthaama. She thus said to Bheem, "Arya, please bring me the gem that Ashvatthaama carries on his head right since birth! A number of times you have fulfilled my vows, brought me succour by fighting for the vows – here is one last request that I would like to be fulfilled."

Bheem immediately set out after the trail of Ashvatthaama, mace in hand. Shrikrishna and Arjun also followed to help.

Ashvatthaama had gone and taken refuge near Bhagwan Vedvyas. He saw Arjun coming from a distance, and sent the *Brahma-shirastra* missile on him. On Shrikrishna's advice, Arjun replied with the same missile, as he too was familiar with it. When the two missiles clashed against each other, such a terrible situation arose that the end of earth seemed to be near; Vedvyas asked Arjun to withdraw his missile. Arjun obliged, but Ashvatthaama just could not. Bhagwan Vyas then advised him, "Ashvatthaama, in any case you are incapable of killing the Pandavs. If you want to live, give up the gem on your head."

Ashvatthaama had no option. He surrendered as Bheem cut off the gem from his head and took it back home to Droupadi.

Legend has it that as Ashvatthaama is one of the seven 'Immortal Beings'*, he still roams on the earth with the ever-flowing wound on his head and seeks oil to put on his head!

|| Consoling the Bereaved ||

Dhritarashtra, Gaandhari and all in the Kourav house were plunged in deep sorrow at the loss of all the Kouravs. They were all weeping with broken hearts. As so many *akshouhinis* of armies were killed, in the Kuru capital every other household had lost either a son, a brother or the husband. Every house was under the pall of grief.

On the sprawling battleground of Kurukshetra, it was nothing short of a graveyard. Thousands of bodies, of those perished in the battle, lay there. Birds of prey, like kites and vultures; and wild dogs, foxes feasted on them.

There was a virtual stampede in Hastinapur. Women looking for their kith and kin among the heaps of corpses rushed to Kurukshetra. Among them was Gaandhari, other women of the Kuru house, accompanied by the blind Dhritarashtra. It was a heart-rending scene. Maharshi Vyas was on hand to console the bereaved. He was joined by Vidur.

The Pandavs, accompanied by Shrikrishna had gone to Dhritarashtra to offer condolences. Each of them would call out his name, and bow humbly before the venerable blind old uncle. The visit by the Pandavs was in fact adding to Dhritarashtra's anger. He was simply fuming with rage. Among the Pandavs, Bheem particularly irritated him, as he had killed the maximum number of his sons. When along with the others, he too came forth to pay his condolences, Dhritarashtra could not contain himself. Somehow controlling the anger within, he asked in a seemingly affectionate tone, "Where is Bheem? I want to meet Bheem first."

Shrikrishna however had seen through Dhritarashtra's show of love; and divining the inner anger, he quickly put forth an iron statue of Bheem before the blind king. Thinking that Bheem was now in

his grasp, Dhritarashtra clasped the statue with so much force that even the iron statue was reduced to fine grains on the spot!

Upon this incident, Shrikrishna gave Dhritarashtra a serious dressing down. He said, "Do not you feel that the evil deeds done by your sons are enough – and so you want to add to that? The war was invited by your sons, with their unjust acts and adamant nature. How are the Pandavs to blame if your sons perished in it?"

Dhritarashtra was feeling a little abashed now. He said,

"I admit, Krishna, that the fault lies entirely with my sons. And I always sided with my sons, denying the rightful claim of the Pandavs. Now there remains nothing for me after the war."

"You should now treat the Pandavs as your own," advised Shrikrishna.

"Yes, indeed. Pandavs are also my blood. It is my family, after all!" said Dhritarashtra, and embraced the Pandavs with affection now. His anguish was reduced a little after this.

Yudhishthir performed all rites for the departed Kourav brethren, and paid them homage.

|| Coronation of Yudhishthir ||

Events in a rapid flow saddened Yudhishthir infinitely. He was extremely disturbed. With so much destruction, so many kinsmen killed, thousands of women and children orphaned, so much blood shed, he felt, 'Is my victory worth all this? Why ascend the throne with roots in such misery?'

He would say, 'I have conquered the whole earth, but there is no joy of victory, there is no succour to the mind. On the contrary, the mere memory of the war burns my mind. As a single spark in a cotton bed slowly burns it all, the memories of war are burning through my being itself. I believe that we have indulged in a major sin, Arjun! In such a frame of mind, I do not feel like becoming king. I would rather bid adieu to you all and go to the woods to undertake penance there.'

This turn of Yudhishthir's mind was quite shocking to Droupadi and the other Pandavs. They together requested him over and over again to change his mind, but Yudhishthir would not give up his decision to go to the woods.

Finally Maharshi Vyas said, "From your speech, I feel, you have forgotten what your kingly duty is, O Yudhishthir! But bear well in mind that your going to the jungle forsaking all worldly things does not befit your stature. Like the bullock that dutifully shoulders the yoke, you should shoulder the responsibility of governing the kingdom. It is your bounded duty to do so. The sacred duties prescribed for those with royal birth are performing yagna, earning knowledge, holding the sceptre, protecting the subjects, earning wealth and donating to the needy. Deviating from any of these duties is destruction. Just as a serpent gobbles up rats living in holes, the king who refuses to put up violent opposition against the enemy is also gobbled up by the enemy. You have forgotten the kingly duties. You better understand it first. But, do you wish to?"

"Yes, Guruji," said Yudhishthir. "I admit that I am quite confused. I need to understand afresh what is to be done and what should not be, what constitutes duties for the king and what does not."

"For that, you must approach *pitamaha* Bheeshma again. He is the only person most capable of explaining to you the crux of your duties as a king," said Maharshi Vyas, asking Yudhishthir to go to Bheeshma.

Lying on his bed of arrows, Bheeshma explained to Yudhishthir the entire gamut of *rajneeti* * – who can be king, why the need for the sceptre, how to avert the onslaught of alien invasion, what the nature of power is, how to select the right chancellor, what constitutes good kingly character, how to recruit proper servants, how statecraft works and what causes the revolution, nature of subjects – all that is needed to be known by the king in order to govern.

As Yudhishthir realized what his duty was, he changed his mind and consented for the coronation.

Afterwards, an auspicious occasion was chosen to crown Yudhishthir as the king. As soon as he took up the sceptre, he appointed the chancellor, various officials and servants of the state. He also instituted various works to keep alive the memory of brave warriors that had fallen in the war – transit houses, food camps and water kiosks. He initiated various public utility works such as wells, ashrams, state highways, *paathshaalas* etc. He also made provisions for the livelihood of the war widows and for the maintenance and caring for orphans.

As time passed, the *uttaraayan* began. *Pitamaha* Bheeshma, who was waiting for this event, concluded his advice to the Pandavs and bid adieu to the world on the Sankranti day, with the name of Shrikrishna on his lips.

|| The Ashvamedh Yagna ||

Yudhishthir performed the last rites of *pitamaha* Bheeshma. With the passing of the elder, he was really very upset and lay under a pall of gloom. Vyas advised him to perform the Ashvamedh yagna.

Yudhishthir made a *sankalp** to perform the yagna. But he did not have the required resources for the rites of sacrifice. The war had emptied his kingdom's coffers. Maharshi Vyas therefore advised him to fetch wealth from the countries at the foot of the Himalayas. Accordingly, all the Pandavs went with a large army to that area and returned from there with their horses, elephants, camels, chariots laden with wealth.

In the interim, between their departure and return however a momentous event had taken place in Hastinapur.

Abhimanyu's wife, Uttara, was pregnant when he had fallen in the war. When she delivered the child after the war, it was a son, but he was stillborn. At this, Kunti, Droupadi, Subhadra – all were aggrieved as this child was the last of the Pandav family tree, and all their hopes were shattered. Their weeping was truly heart-rending. Hearing it, Shrikrishna summoned all his divine powers and filled the child with life once again.

When the child began moving its hand and feet again, the womenfolk were relieved. By then, the Pandavs also returned from their treasure-hunt. They were overjoyed to hear this news and celebrated the new birth in a grand style. The heir to the Pandav kingdom was named Parikshita.

Parikshita's birth was followed by the hectic activities of the Ashvamedh yagna. Sages and ascetics, pandits and kings from near and far, assembled for the yagna. Hastinapur was filled with thousands of guests. The Ashvamedh horse bearing all the prescribed qualities was prepared and decorated. While the yagna began at the hands of Yudhishthir, protection of the roaming horse of the yagna was Arjun's responsibility.

The horse was set going. It went from kingdom to kingdom, and everywhere it was welcomed. Nobody wanted to stop it. Only at Manipur, Babhruvaahan stopped the horse and would not let it go. He did not recognize the accompanying Arjun, and took up a firm position to fight. It would have been a son-and-father fight, for he was none but Arjun's son from Uloopi. When he was told of his birth history, he put down the bow and greeted his father. He also let the horse go.

The horse further went to many countries, kingdoms. But none dared to stop him; for such was the impact of the valour of Arjun, the archer. None dared to challenge him.

After having toured all the countries, the horse returned to Hastinapur.

The finale of the Ashvamedh yagna was celebrated with much enthusiasm.

‖ Taking to the Woods ‖

One day, Dhritarashtra said to Yudhishthir, "Allow us to go to the woods now, son."

"Why do you wish to go to the woods, may I ask?"

"My end is near. I wish to spend the final days in the ways of God, away from the worldly temptations."

Dhritarashtra's proposal was also seconded by Maharshi Vyas. Yudhishthir reluctantly permitted the leaving of the elders for the woods.

Along with Dhritarashtra, Gaandhari, Kunti, Vidur – the elders, and Sanjay, prepared to go to the woods.

The citizens of Hastinapur were plunged in gloom.

Besides the Pandavs, a huge crowd of people went outside the city limits to see the elders off.

Dhritarashtra was walking with his hand on Vidur's shoulder for support. He paused, and turning to the people, said,

"Dear people, now you better return. Now let us go our way. Please do not tempt us with your love any more."

The Pandavs, as well as the citizens returned to the capital. The group of elders however slowly made their way to the woods, holding and supporting each other.

Days passed. But the memory of the elders in the woods still used to disturb Pandavs. Particularly, Droupadi wanted to meet Kunti very much. Therefore, one day, they decided to go to the woods to call on the elders. Accordingly, they went to the jungle. They had their meeting, and were happy. But in this meeting, Vidur was nowhere; he had already reached the great beyond.

As Dhritarashtra and Kunti desired, Vyas created the appearance of Karna and all the Kouravs one day. The parents were relieved with this one-time reappearance of the dear ones. Following that, all womenfolk of the Kourav household sacrificed their bodies into the river Ganga.

The Pandavs returned home to Hastinapur. They began the routine of looking after the state but with a heavy heart. Some more uneventful days passed, and one day Sage Narad brought them the news.

'As they were returning after bathing in the river Ganga, the trio of Dhritarashtra, Gaandhari and Kunti – their bodies enfeebled by constant fasts – were caught in the wild fire and were reduced to ashes'.

The Pandavs were very much grieved by the news.

‖ The End of Krishna Avataar ‖

Yudhishthir ruled his kingdom from Hastinapur for 36 long years. His subjects were a happy lot.

But Yudhishthir had premonitions of impending doom, and the Pandavs did get a shockingly painful news then.

As Sages Vishwamitra, Kanva and Narad were entering Dwaraka, some Yadav youths had the perverse idea of ridiculing the senior sages. They dressed up a young Yadav 'Samb' in a blouse-and-saree and taking this 'woman' up to the sages they asked, "What shall this woman deliver – a boy or a girl?"

Vishwamitra saw through their game. He was quite angry and said in curse, "This woman shall deliver an iron pounder; and it shall destroy the entire Andhak family tree of yours!"

Indeed, by the curse, Samb delivered a heavy iron bar. Seeing it, the Yadav chief Agrasen was terrified. He arranged to have the bar powdered, and drowned the whole thing into the sea.

But this did not put an end to the fate awaiting the Yadavs. Yadav youths had their fill of intoxicants and began to fight among themselves. They were bent on killing each other.

Seeing the youth of his family go astray in such a manner, Shrikrishna uprooted some grass on the seashore and threw the grass-straws at them. Miraculously, the straws turned into iron rods and went on killing one Yadav youth after another. The destruction of the Yadavs was quite widespread.

Balram used his powers of Yoga to lay down his life.

Shrikrishna then went to a forest and sat meditating under a tree, his foot placed sole upwards. A passing hunter mistook it for the mouth of a deer and shot an arrow at it. This gave enough cause for Shrikrishna to end his life-journey and forsaking the human body, he ended his Avataar.

✥ ✥ ✥

|| The Final Journey ||

Learning of Shrikrishna's end, the Pandavs were naturally aggrieved to the extreme. Yudhishthir then said to his brothers and wife,

"It is time now for us also to begin the final journey."

All of them agreed.

And then they began the final arrangements:

Shrikrishna's grandson Vraj was the only survivor of the mighty Vrishnee* clan. He was given the kingdom of Indraprastha. Parikshita was crowned the king at Hastinapur. Subhadra was kept behind to look after the two young princes.

And then once more, all the Pandavs and Droupadi shed their royal garments and ornaments, and wore tree-bark clothes in their place.

Their citizens bade them adieu with very heavy heart. Then the Pandavs began their journey. This was the journey of no return. Now they were ultimately headed towards the final destination of their lives.

As they walked the long road, Droupadi collapsed and breathed her last.

Bheem was surprised. He asked Yudhishthir,

"Why did she have to be the first to die?"

"She was abiding by her duties as the wife well; but in the heart of hearts, she loved Arjun more than the others. The fall of hers is the end-result of that little partiality which she showed in the matter of love."

After a little distance, Sahadeo collapsed and died. He was followed in death by Nakul and Arjun. Again on the query of Bheem, Yudhishthir told him, "Sahadeo was proud of his wisdom, and Nakul thought that there was nobody as handsome as him. They both

suffered. Arjun too had been affected by pride for his bravery. Moreover, he went on taking vows such as: I shall finish off the enemies within the day; and these vows were never kept. This is not only not right, it also brings ignominy to the art of archery. Therefore, Arjun had to fall. And now it is your turn, Bheem. You, too, were not free from pride about your strength."

Bheem was the next Pandav to fall and die.

Now it was only Yudhishthir, and the dog who had been accompanying them right since the beginning of their journey. They were entitled to enter the heavens with their bodies, without relinquishing them.

Indra, the Lord of heavens, himself came to receive Yudhishthir. He offered the chariot to Yudhishthir, asking him to come to the heavens in it. But Yudhishthir refused to get into the chariot alone, unless the accompanying dog also was admitted with him. Indra declined, on the grounds that only those that have enough merit are admissible; Yudhishthir offered to give half of his own merit to the dog so that it also could be admitted.

Such was the thorough righteousness of Yudhishthir that Yamadharma, the Deity of Beyond, was astonished. He gave up the form of the dog that he had assumed and manifested himself. He was all praise for Yudhishthir.

After this, ascending the chariot of Indra, Yudhishthir reached the heavens without losing the human body.

Thus a great saga of the Kuru dynasty ended.

GLOSSARY

Arghya: An offering with dedication, even of water.

Ashta-Vasus: The eight *Vasus*, a class of deities.

Astra: Missile

Bharat: Name of a king, Dushyant's son from which the name of our country 'Bhaarat' is derived.

Guru-dakshina: Offering to the guru at the conclusion of studies.

Adnyat: (incognito) where a person's name, family etc. is unknown (kept secret).

Krishnadvaipaayan: Literally meaning, dark and born on an island (Name of Maharshi Vyas).

Maharathi: A category of warriors: Rathi> Atirathi > Maharathi

Niyog: Fertilizing by a person other than spouse (Test-tube baby-like practice).

Pana: Condition for winning a bride in *svayamvar*.

Praja: Literally, children, offspring. Subject-people, citizens.

Prahar: One eighth of full day, approx. three hours.

Rajneeti: The do's and don'ts for kings.

Sandhya: A daily ritual prayer, particularly for Brahmins.

Sankalp: Formal resolution.

Sarp-satra: Parikshita's sacrifice of serpents, begun as revenge.

Shakti: A special weapon, particularly missile by an arrow.

Shanti: Peace

Seven Immortals:

अश्वत्थामा बलिर्व्यासः हनुमांश्च बिभीषणः। कृपःपरशुरामःच सप्तैते चिरजीविनः॥

–Ashvatthama, Bali, Vyas, Maruti, Bibheeshan, Kripa and Parshuram are believed to be the seven immortal beings.

Svayamvar: Custom of the bride choosing her own groom.

Uttaraayan: Apparent Northward movement of the Sun.

Vanvaas: Exile into forest.

Vrishnee: Family/dynasty of Krishna (like Pandavs are *Kurus*)

Vyadh: A person living by hunting.

Yaksha: A heavenly being.

Yojan: Measure of distance in old days, app.14/15 kms. (9 miles).

Ramayan is a priceless heritage of India.
Lord Ramchandra, by his righteous conduct,
has created here an ideal of the King,
of King-like behaviour and of running the state–
not just for Indians but for the entire mankind.
Despite being superhuman,
Shriram, with Seeta and Lakshman, went through
joys and sufferings of the common man.
With the listening and reading
of their account going on constantly,
Ram-Janaki and Lakshman
have won an intimate place
in the hearts of the Indians for ever.
As long as Man lives
and has speech and language,
Ramayan lives on...

|| Ramayan ||

–Raja Mangalvedhekar